Cambridge English

FUN
for **Flyers**

Student's Book
Third edition

Anne Robinson
Karen Saxby

Cambridge University Press
www.cambridge.org/elt

Cambridge English Language Assessment
www.cambridgeenglish.org

Information on this title: www.cambridge.org/9781107444836

© Cambridge University Press 2015

First published 2006
Second edition 2010
Third edition 2015
20 19 18 17 16 15 14 13 12 11 10 9

Printed in Italy by Rotolito Lombarda S.p.A.

A catalogue record for this publication is available from the British Library

ISBN 978-1107-44483-6 Student's Book with audio and online activities
ISBN 978-1107-44484-3 Teacher's Book with audio
ISBN 978-1107-44485-0 Class Audio CDs (2)
ISBN 978-1107-48407-8 Presentation Plus DVD-ROM

Download the audio at www.cambridge.org/funfor

The authors and publishers would like to thank the ELT professionals who commented on the material at different stages of its development.

The authors are grateful to Niki Donnelly of Cambridge University Press.

Anne Robinson would like to give special thanks to Adam Evans, and her parents Margaret and Jim and to many, many teachers and students who have inspired her along the way. Special thanks to Cristina and Victoria for their help, patience and enthusiasm. And in memory of her brother Dave.

Karen Saxby would like to give special thanks to everyone she has worked with at Cambridge Assessment since the birth of YLE! She would particularly like to mention Frances, Felicity and Ann Kelly. She would also like to acknowledge the enthusiasm of all the teachers she has met through her work in this field. And lastly, Karen would like to say a big thank you to her sons, Tom and William, for bringing constant FUN and creative thinking to her life and work.

Editorial work by Bridget Kelly

Cover design by Crush Creative

Book design and page make-up by emc design Ltd

The authors and publishers are grateful to the following illustrators:
Akbar Ali (The Organisation) pp. 6 (B), 7 (R), 10, 23 (B), 24 (B), 25, 35 (B), 39 (B), 44 (B), 52, 81, 85 (T), 104 (R), 105 (B), 114, 115; Laetitia Aynié (Sylvie Poggio Artists Agency) pp. 12, 40 (BL), 73, 97, 101 (BR); David Banks pp. 65, 79, 99; Bridget Dowty (Graham-Cameron Illustration) pp. 33 (T), 39 (T), 96; Andy Elkerton (Sylvie Poggio Artists Agency) pp. 14, 19, 34 (TL); Chris Embleton-Hall (Advocate Art) pp. 20, 22, 54 (B), 75 (CR); Pablo Gallego (Beehive Illustration) pp. 13 (B), 21 (B), 27 (T), 32, 57, 91, 100 (BR), 101 (C), 126, 128 (BR); Daniela Geremia (Beehive Illustration) pp. 8 (C), 18 (B), 36 (B), 69 (B), 106 (T); John Haslam pp. 7 (BC), 8 (T), 13 (T), 14 (TL), 16, 17 (B), 46, 50 (B), 58, 59 (C), 68 (B), 82 (B), 90 (C), 110, 111 (T); Brett Hudson (Graham-Cameron Illustration) pp. 48 (B), 49 (TR), 106 (R), 107 (B); Nigel Kitching (Sylvie Poggio Artists Agency) pp. 26 (T), 29 (T), 94, 105 (R); Gustavo Mazali (Beehive Illustration) pp. 9, 14 (B), 17 (T), 21 (T), 44 (T), 45, 50 (T), 54 (T), 59 (T), 79, 82 (T), 98, 104 (TR), 112 (CR), 122, 124, 126, 128 (T); Nina de Polonia (Advocate Art) pp. 15, 24 (TR), 35 (T), 40 (T), 48 (T), 56 (C), 61 (TR), 69 (T), 74, 90 (BL); Pulsar Studios (Beehive Illustration) pp. 53, 64 (BR), 95 (T), 109, 119, 121; Anthony Rule pp. 5, 6 (T), 7 (BR), 17 (BL), 24 (R), 29 (B), 31 (B), 33 (B), 42, 47 (B), 49 (B), 51, 52, 56 (T), 59 (B), 61 (BR), 70 (T), 75 (BR), 76, 77 (BR), 85 (BR), 90 (T), 92 (T), 95 (R), 100 (T), 106 (TR), 111 (BR), 112 (T), 116 (T), 123 (BR) 125 (BR), 127 (TR); Pip Sampson pp. 11, 23 (T), 28, 37, 55, 62, 63, 66, 67, 68 (T), 86, 87, 107 (T), 127 (C); Will Saxby p. 73 (TR); Melanie Sharp (Sylvie Poggio Artists Agency) pp. 18 (T), 26 (B), 27 (B), 30, 31 (T), 34 (TC), 47 (T), 70 (B), 71, 72, 75 (T), 84, 92 (BR), 93, 102, 103, 113, 116 (B), 117; Emily Skinner (Graham-Cameron Illustration) pp. 88 (T), 89 (C), 108; Lisa Smith p. 36; Jo Taylor p. 42; Theresa Tibbetts (Beehive Illustration) p. 92 (TL); Tatio Viana (Advocate Art) pp. 38, 41, 47 (C), 64 (T), 76, 77 (T), 88 (B), 89 (T), 99, 106 (B), 123 (T), 125

The authors and publishers acknowledge the following sources of copyright material and are grateful for the permissions granted. While every effort has been made, it has not always been possible to identify the sources of all the material used, or to trace all copyright holders. If any omissions are brought to our notice, we will be happy to include the appropriate acknowledgements on reprinting.

Sound recordings by dsound, London

Contents

1	Hello again	6
2	Wearing and carrying	8
3	Spots and stripes	10
4	My friends and my pets	12
5	About animals	14
6	My things	16
7	Moving and speaking	18
8	School subjects	20
9	In my classroom	22
10	Clothes, animals and school	24
11	Visiting different places	26
12	A journey into space	28
13	What horrible weather!	30
14	Are you hungry? Thirsty?	32
15	What's for dinner?	34
16	Let's have a picnic!	36
17	A day's work	38
18	Time and work	40
19	Answer my questions	42
20	Calling and sending	44
21	The time of the year	46
22	Important numbers	48
23	World, weather, work	50
24	Leaving and arriving	52
25	What shall we do next?	54
26	Where can we go on holiday?	56
27	It's the holidays! Bye!	58
28	I want to win!	60
29	Doing sport! Having fun!	62
30	Summer and winter sports	64

31	Here and there	66
32	Where?	68
33	At the hospital	70
34	John stays in hospital	72
35	What's it made of?	74
36	Silver, plastic, glass, gold	76
37	Exciting days!	78
38	Famous people	80
39	In villages and towns	82
40	What a strange planet!	84
41	Meet the pirate actors	86
42	Holiday news	88
43	Have you ever ...?	90
44	What has just happened?	92
45	Talking about the time	94
46	We're all at home today	96
47	I will or perhaps I won't	98
48	Doing different things	100
49	Busy families	102
50	On TV	104
51	Here's my news	106
52	What a lot of questions!	108
53	Finding your way	110
54	Let's have some fun!	112
55	If I feel bored	114
56	Fun and games	116
	Pairwork activities	118–129
	Unit wordlist	130–141
	List of irregular verbs	142–143

1 Hello again

A Look at the picture. Where are these? Draw lines.

the sky   the seat   the skateboard   the backpack   the roof
the bicycle   the grass   the sunglasses

B Say how the pictures are different.

C Look at the picture in B and read. Write yes or no.

Examples

One of the boys is riding a blue bicycle. ...yes...

There are pink and white flowers in the grass. ...no...

1   Only one of the backpacks is pink. ....

2   There is a yellow moon on the girl's skateboard. ....

3   You can see a lot of grey clouds in the sky. ....

4   Both seats in this playground are brown. ....

5   There is a lorry in the road behind the school. ....

6   You can see more than one cow in the field under the rainbow. ....

D ▶ Listen and write the answers.

	Robert's favourite game	
Example	Name of game:	Silver Moon
1	When got this game:	last ....
2	Played this game with:	his ....
3	Name of alien in game:	....
4	Colour of alien's feet:	....
5	Alien likes finding:	....

E Find the answer to each question. Draw lines.

1   How do you get to school in the morning?

2   Do you play video games in your classroom sometimes?

3   What do you like talking about with your friends?

4   Where do you like going with your friends?

5   Which clothes do you like wearing most?

6   What's your favourite colour?

a   I think it's blue, but I like black, too.

b   I like jeans and T-shirts best.

c   Our favourite place is the playground.

d   We can't do that in the lessons.

e   Television and people in our class at school.

f   I ride my bicycle, but not every day.

g   No, my friend likes yellow most.

F Let's say!

round clouds and brown cows!

7

2 'Wearing and carrying'

A Write letters to make words under the pictures. Where do we wear these? Draw lines.

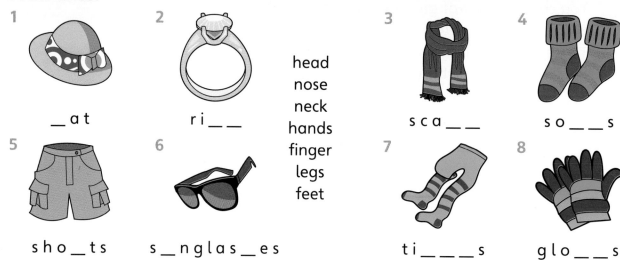

1 _ a t

2 r i _ _

head
nose
neck
hands
finger
legs
feet

3 s c a _ _

4 s o _ _ _ s

5 s h o _ t s

6 s _ n g l a s _ e s

7 t i _ _ _ _ s

8 g l o _ _ s

B Read the sentences and write the correct words from the box.

a watch   an umbrella   gloves   a rucksack   pockets   a coat   a belt
shorts   a backpack   a handbag   suitcases   a uniform   tights

1 People can carry things on their back in this.   a rucksack / ....

2 You wear this over other clothes when you go outside.   ....

3 Women often carry this. They put things like pens and keys in it.   ....

4 Some school children have to wear this when they go to school.   ....

5 Some girls and women wear these on their legs when it's cold.   ....

6 When you want to know the time, look at this.   ....

7 These are like jeans or trousers but much shorter!   ....

8 When it rains, you can open this so you don't get wet.   ....

9   People carry things in these when they are travelling. Some
      have little wheels.   ....

10   Some people wear this round the top of their trousers or skirt.   ....

11   We put these on our hands in cold weather.   ....

12   If you're wearing trousers, you can keep small things in these.   ....

C Look and read. Circle the correct word.

1   The queen is wearing a very pretty *necklace* / *belt*.

2   *Three / four* long, thin flags are flying in the wind.

3   One person is carrying a big plate with *fruit / pasta* on it.

4   The man who's playing music is wearing funny orange *tights / gloves*.

5   You can see a large *round / square* table in the castle garden.

6   The king has a wonderful gold *crown / hat* on the top of his head.

D Who are the people at the castle? Listen and draw lines.

Mary

Peter

Robert

....

Helen

Sarah

....

Michael

Harry

E Listen again. Answer the questions.

1   What is the name of the castle?

2   Who listens to the king's secrets?

3   Who is the queen's best friend?

4   Who is the important letter for?

F Play the game! Why are you together?

3 'Spots and stripes'

A Look and read. Write yes or no.

Examples

One boy in the picture is wearing a scarf and gloves. ...yes....

A happy girl is sitting next to the person who's talking on the phone. ...no....

Questions

1   The woman with two boys is pushing more than three suitcases. ....

2   A large information screen is on the wall above the toy bears. ....

3   The man with the beard is writing something in his newspaper. ....

4   The bags by the man's feet have got stars on them. ....

5   The time on the clock is half past three. ....

6   Passengers are going through the door of the biggest plane. ....

7   The boy who is taking off a striped jacket is listening to music. ....

B ▶ Look at the picture in A. Listen and colour and draw and write.

C Talk about the flags in the first picture.

D Complete the sentences about the second picture. Use 1 or 2 words.

Example   There's one boat and it's got three green flags with ....*sharks*.... on them.

1   The man with the beard isn't wearing .... on his feet.

2   The boys are carrying large .... in their right hands.

3   The child who's wearing pink and yellow .... is cleaning the boat.

4   The .... is coming out from behind the clouds.

5   The towel on the boy's shoulder has blue and .... stripes on it.

E Look at the pictures. What differences can you see?

F Can you find the picture I've written about?

4 'My friends and my pets'

A Let's talk about your friends and family.

1 Who lives in your house? Who's the oldest person in your house?

2 Has anyone in your family got your name too?

3 Who do you sit next to at school? Do you always sit in the same seat?

4 Which friends do you see at the weekend? What do you do with your friends at the weekend?

5 Tell me about your best friend. What does she/he look like?
Tell me about her/his hobbies.

B ▶ What does Holly say about her friends?
Listen, write names, then draw lines.

1 ...... Jane ......   a also has guitar lessons.
2 ....   b is in the same class.
3 ....   c is Holly's cousin.
4 ....   d is Holly's best friend.
5 ....   e likes the same music.
6 ....   f is very funny.
7 ....   g goes sailing too.
8 ....   h is a loud singer.

C Now write the names of people you know.

1 .... likes the music I like.

2 .... is the funniest person in this class.

3 .... is a really great singer.

4 .... is very good at sport.

D Read the email and write the missing words. Write one word on each line.

Hi David!

Come and see our new house next week! Monday's

Example ....*the*....... best day.

1 It's quite easy to get here .... bus because it stops on the corner of our street. You can also meet our new pet! It's bright green and really sweet but it's much naughtier

2 .... your pet rabbit! It steals grapes and bits

3 .... bread from the kitchen table sometimes!

4 .... the weather's OK, we can watch the football

5 match in King's Park. .... is your favourite football team?

See you!
Sally

E ▶ Listen and write the names.

Monday – Go to friend's house!
1 Name: ....*Sally*...........
2 Bus stop is in: .... Street
3 Sally's house is in: .... Road
4 Name of house: ....
5 Sally's dog's name: ....
6 Sally's parrot's name: ....

F Where are the 'h's?

13

5 About animals

A How do they move? Write the animals below each word.

> kangaroo   bat   fish   mouse   bird   crocodile   goat   dolphin

run	fly	jump	swim	hop
mouse				

B Look and read. Choose the correct word and write it on the line.

butterflies
a camel
dinosaurs
a bee
an octopus
swans
~~a rabbit~~

1 This wild animal usually has grey fur and when it feels frightened, it hops away very quickly.   ...... *a rabbit* ......

2 This is an insect that works hard to make honey.   ....

3 This animal has a long neck and can carry heavy bags for a long time in hot, dry places.   ....

4 These big birds are usually white. They have long necks and live near rivers and lakes.   ....

5 This animal lives in the sea and has eight long arms.   ....

6 These have wings with lots of different colours on them. They fly and sit on plants and flowers.   ....

7 These animals are extinct now so we can only see them in cartoons, films, story books or museums.   ....

C Choose the right words and write them on the lines.

Example	Dinosaurs _____*lived*_____ on our planet 150,000,000 years ago! The first dinosaurs		living	lives	lived
1	_____ like big lizards. Many of them	1	looks	looked	looking
2	had short tails, big heads _____ walked on four legs. Most dinosaurs were herbivores, which means that they only ate plants. Some of these dinosaurs were very	2	and	because	than
3	_____ but other kinds of dinosaur were bigger and heavier and were carnivores, which means that they ate meat. Dinosaurs	3	small	smaller	smallest
4	lived _____ warm forests where	4	to	in	from
5	there were lots and lots _____ plants and water. But about 60,000,000 years ago,	5	off	out	of
6	some people say _____ weather on our planet suddenly got colder and drier.	6	the	one	those
7	Many plants _____ dinosaurs liked to eat stopped growing, which was a terrible problem for these animals, so soon dinosaurs disappeared too.	7	what	that	who
8	Today, people sometimes _____ dinosaur teeth in rocks or under the ground. Dinosaurs are now extinct, but you can	8	finds	found	find
9	learn about _____ in special science museums or when you watch dinosaur films	9	they	their	them
10	_____ TV.	10	at	by	on

D Do you know the missing word?

| Lots _____ dinosaurs   a story _____ a dolphin |

1	all kinds _____ bats	4	this part _____ the story
2	a book _____ the jungle	5	a cartoon _____ wild animals
3	a pair _____ wings	6	a song _____ a dolphin

E Play the game! Dolphins or bats?

6 My things

A   What are these? Write words on the lines next to the pictures.

A .... *a sweater* ....

B ▶ Listen. Which animal is on each thing in A? Write a letter (A–H).

A   B   C   D

E   F   G   H

C ▶ **Match, then colour the two parts of the sentences.**

A	Betty's mother decided to buy this sweater		from a shop in the mountains.
B	Her friend Mary chose this and		on her camping holiday last summer.
C	Her mother got her this in January		Betty's fingers and hands don't get cold.
D	Her grandmother made these so		at the zoo shop last year.
E	Her cousin, Ben, bought her this because		Betty always brushes her hair with it.
F	Betty carried her things in this		Betty loves these sea animals.

D **Ask and answer questions about some more of Betty's things.**

A **Betty's keyboard**

Colour	silver
When/get	last Saturday
New/old	new
Who/gave	aunt
Where/now	upstairs

B **Betty's violin**

New/old	old
Where/now	downstairs
Who/gave	grandfather
When/get	last birthday
Colour	light brown

E **Let's do an animal quiz!**

7 Moving and speaking

A Write **eyes, ears, mouth, nose** or **hands** next to the words.

bounce	hands	smell		catch		cry	
shout		see		cook		whistle	
carry		throw		hear		whisper	
speak		call		watch		sing	
push		laugh		pull		hold	

B Complete each sentence with a word from the word box.

> whisper   hear   believe   Describe   guess   decide

1 Could you speak more loudly, please? I can't .... you.
2 .... your school uniform to me. What does it look like?
3 My friends sometimes .... secrets to me in class!
4 I can't .... what to wear today! My new dress or jeans?
5 Dad doesn't always .... me when I say my bedroom's tidy!
6 Can you .... the name of my favourite band?

C Look at the pictures and tell the story.

1

2

3

4

5

D Read the story. Choose a word from the box. Write the correct word next to numbers 1–5.

I'm Helen. I live in the ......city...... but last August I visited my new school friend, David, who lives on a farm in the north of the country. His dad, William, is a famous (1) ...., but he's a farmer too! I saw lots of cows and other (2) .... there, but I remember Pirate, the black and white sheep dog, most.

Early one morning, David's dad came into the kitchen. 'The sheep in the west field aren't there now!' he said. 'I must find them. Come and help me!' David and I jumped up and followed him outside. We all (3) .... up into his big old green truck. Pirate jumped in too.

William drove the truck up the hill. Suddenly, Pirate got very (4) .... William stopped the truck and shouted, 'Go, Pirate! Find the sheep!' Pirate jumped out of the truck and ran behind some trees. A minute later, we saw him again. The clever dog ran round and round the sheep to make them come back down into the west field.

David's dad (5) .... loudly and called, 'Well done, Pirate!'

Pirate worked very hard that day. 'He's tired,' I whispered to David after dinner. 'He ran a long way today.' But Pirate wasn't too tired to eat some of his favourite cookies that evening!

Example

city   cloudy   whistled   actor   wings   climbed   animals   sausages   excited   painted

---

Now choose the best name for this story. Tick (✔) one box.

Pirate loses his biscuits ☐

Pirate helps on the farm ☐

Pirate drives a truck ☐

E Write words to complete the sentences.

8 'School subjects'

A Write a, e, i, o or u.

<u>A</u> r t

G _ _ g r _ p h y

H _ s t _ r y

S p _ r t

L _ n g _ _ g _ s

M _ t h s

M _ s _ c

S c _ _ n c _

B Choose the correct words from A and write them on the lines.

1 Teachers might tell you famous facts about the past in this lesson. ....

2 You sometimes have to add several numbers together in this subject. ....

3 When you study this, you might learn about rocks or caves. ....

4 You talk and listen to your partner and learn new words in these lessons. ....

5 Students learn to play different instruments in this class. ....

C Complete these sentences about Art.

artists
draw
paintings
drawing
paints

1 Your teacher shows you how to .... with pencils in this lesson.

2 If you are very good at .... you usually enjoy doing this!

3 You sometimes use brushes, clean water and .... in this class.

4 In this subject, some students look at .... by famous .... Do you?

D Write sentences about Sport and Science.

....

....

E ▶ Listen and write.

	Monday	
Example	Meet in:	the town ....square.......
1	See art by:	Alex ....
2	Bus number:	....
3	Sport to read about:	....
4	Time parents should come:	....
5	For lunch, can have:	....

F Read the email and write the missing words.
Write one word on each line.

To [   ]
Subject [   ]

Hi Robert,

Example I ....'m....... sending you this email because you weren't at school today.

1 In Mr Park's class, we had .... read a text about pyramids.
2 It was very interesting! Some of them are 5000 years ....!
3 Did you know that? For homework, we must .... out more
4 things about them. So, look for pictures .... the pyramids or read more about them on your computer.

You could write something about them too if
5 you like, but not more .... 100 words.

See you tomorrow!
William

G Answer the questions. Then choose the best answers for the conversation.

9 'In my classroom'

A Find the two halves of the sentences.

1   Glue: When you break a cup or plate,
2   Scissors: They are usually made of metal and
3   A dictionary: When you don't understand a word,
4   A bin: When something is old and you don't want it,
5   A calendar: To help you to remember a special day,

a   you can use them to cut thin card or plastic.
b   look in this to find out what it means.
c   you can try to repair it with this.
d   draw a circle round the date on this.
e   it's a good idea to put it in one of these.

B ▶ Listen and tick (✔) the box.

Example **Where can William sit now?**

A ☐   B ✔   C ☐

1   What's the first lesson today?

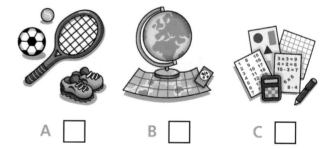

A ☐   B ☐   C ☐

2   What should the students take to their art class?

A ☐   B ☐   C ☐

3   What did William forget to bring to school?

A ☐   B ☐   C ☐

4   Where should the students put their dictionaries?

A ☐   B ☐   C ☐

5   What kind of competition is it?

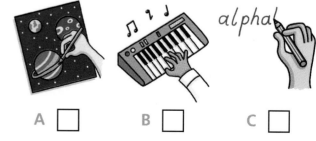

A ☐   B ☐   C ☐

C Look at the pictures and write ee or ea in the words!

1   Miss Sl e e p is showing the qu__ __ n all the gr__ __ n tr__ __s this w__ __ k.
2   Pl __ __ se make sure your volleyball t__ __m have got c l__ __ n j __ __ ns on!
3   It's r__ __lly __ __ sy for Tom to st__ __ l __ __ch l__ __ f from the tree.
4   In my dr__ __m I had a m__ __ l on the b__ __ ch with a s__ __ monster!
5   Tell the h__ __dteacher that her cakes and brown br__ __d are r__ __dy!
6   We can't carry the h__ __ vy tr __ __sure in this wet w__ __ther.

D Ask and answer questions about different classes.

Michael's class

Name/teacher?	....
How many desks?	....
What/children studying?	....
What/on wall?	....
Lesson easy/difficult?	....

Holly's class

Name/teacher?	....
How many desks?	....
What/children studying?	....
What/on wall?	....
Lesson easy/difficult?	....

E Let's do a pair dictation!

10 'Clothes, animals and school'

A ▶ Listen and write.

	Our school trip!		
Example	Place:	...........butterfly.......... farm	
1	Day of trip:	....	
2	Went there by:	....	
3	Left school at:	.... o'clock	
4	Most unusual animal:	a black	
5	Had a picnic lunch by:	a	

B Talk about your school trip!

C Look at the picture and write words. Find 16 more things that begin with the same first letter!

a apple and *animal,* ....

b book and ....

c comic and ....

d dress and ....

f finger and ....

g gloves and ....

h hair and ....

i information and ....

l lizard and ....

m mouth and ....

n necklace and ....

p parrot and ....

r ring and ....

s scissors and ....

t teacher and ....

u uniform and ....

w water and ....

D Look and read. Choose the correct words and write them on the lines.

languages   sunglasses   a necklace   a dictionary

You can use this to see the spellings and meanings of words. ....*a dictionary*.......

a swan

fur

1 In your music lessons, you might listen to people playing these. ....

2 Some people wear these because they don't like looking at bright lights. ....

3 Birds and butterflies use these to help them fly high in the air. ....

Science

4 These are the words and ways people speak in different parts of the world. ....

wings

5 This is perhaps the best animal to ride if you want to cross a desert! ....

6 In this subject you might learn how metals change when they get hot. ....

a pocket

7 This is the soft coat that animals like rabbits and kittens have on their bodies. ....

tights

8 If you are wearing jeans, you can put your key or phone in this. ....

a crown

9 Older students go to this place to learn subjects like History or Science. ....

10 A king might wear this on his head when he is with other important people. ....

instruments   a camel   a college   an insect

E Play the game. What's my word?

11 'Visiting different places'

A Read the sentences then complete words 2–10 in the S puzzle.

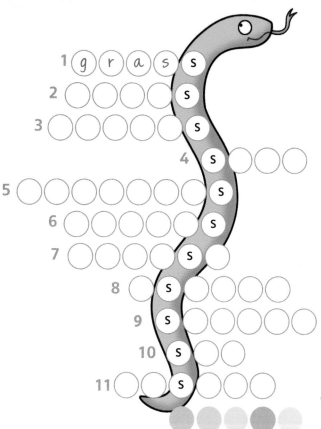

1 g r a s s
2
3
4
5
6
7
8
9
10
11

1 This is green and you can usually find it in gardens. Cows eat it!

2 You can walk up these because they're lower than mountains.

3 You find these on farms and some farmers grow vegetables in them.

4 This is usually yellow. It's under your feet when you walk on the beach.

5 People live and work in these places. They're like towns but smaller.

6 You see these on all kinds of plants. They sometimes fall off trees.

7 You can find thousands of tall trees in this place.

8 There is water all round this place so you need a boat to get to it.

9 Most of these are really pretty and you find them on the beach or at the bottom of the sea.

10 When it rains, this is grey and has lots of clouds in it.

B ▶ Listen and colour and draw and write.

26

C What is Katy saying to her friend, Dan? Choose the best answer.

Dan: Hello, Katy! How are you? Is everything OK?

Katy: .....B.....

1 Dan: Are you camping next to a lake again?

   Katy: ....

2 Dan: Who else is there with you?

   Katy: ....

3 Dan: Are there any wild animals?

   Katy: ....

4 Dan: Where do you sleep at night?

   Katy: ....

5 Dan: What about the weather?

   Katy: ....

Dan: ....   Katy: ....

A I'd like to take the dog for a walk.
B We're having a wonderful time, thanks! Example
C My parents but there are several other people here, too.
D It changes from cold at night to very hot in the day.
E We've got tents that have special camping beds inside them.
F But the water's warm because it was so sunny.
G That's right. This one's in Yellow Hill Desert, actually.
H I can only see our camels which are really fun to ride!

D What's in each rucksack?

gloves   sweater
map   hat   T-shirt
camera   dictionary
chocolate   chess game
torch   sunglasses
phone   umbrella
cold water   blanket

E Play the game! Moving dictation.

A Complete the sentences about the picture.

1   An astronaut is jumping off the top of the ...._stairs_........ .
2   Two of the astronauts are playing .... near the strange tree.
3   The rocket door is .... now.
4   A robot with a square .... is watching TV inside the rocket.
5   One of the planets is .... than the other two.
6   The trees have got leaves that look like .... hands.
7   The .... under the rocket looks a bit like sand.

stairs   dark   open   chess   larger   head   later   golf   little   ground   air

B ▶ Listen and write names.

....

C What differences can you see?

D Read the text. Choose the right words and write them on the lines.

Our planet

Example	The planet we live ......on...... is called 'Earth'. Earth is one of the		on	at	in
1	eight planets .... move round and round the sun.	1	what	who	that
2	Until .... twentieth century, we didn't	2	all	the	one
3	have .... really good maps of our	3	lots	any	no
4	planet. But now, we can .... pictures of Earth with special cameras in space and making maps is easy!	4	take	taking	took
5	.... of our planet has water on it so, in	5	Most	Every	Many
6	pictures, Earth often .... like a big blue and white ball!	6	looking	look	looks
	But pictures of Earth don't only help us to make				
7	maps. When we look at ...., we can	7	they	their	them
8	also learn a .... about the Earth's environment and weather.	8	too	lot	some
9	Travelling in space .... watching other planets helps us to learn more about Earth, too.	9	and	because	but
10	.... you like to be an astronaut one day?	10	Can	May	Would

E ▶ Listen and write names, then colour the planets.

The sun   Earth   Venus   Neptune

Mars   Mercury   Uranus   Saturn   Jupiter

F Answer questions about our planet.

Earth			
What/colour?	blue and white	How long/take/ go round/sun?	365 days, 6 hours and 16 minutes
What/temperature?	about 14°C		
Has/rings?	no	How many/moons?	1

G Let's find out about other planets!

29

13 What horrible weather!

A Find the weather words.

warmcloudswetwindydryrainhotsunnystormfoggysnowcoldicerainbowtemperature

B ▶ **Listen. Use words from A to complete the sentences.**

1 Alex and his friend can't play volleyball if it starts to ....*rain*........ .
2 Dad and Daisy are talking about the noisy .... last night.
3 Mr and Mrs Lime can see a beautiful .... in the sky.
4 Dad wants Helen to remember there might be .... on the ground.
5 Mum says it's dangerous to drive quickly in .... weather.
6 John wants to go out and play in the ....

If it snows, I'd like to ....

C ▶ **Look at the picture. Listen and draw lines.**

Holly   Harry   Sarah

George   Emma   William   Betty

D Look at the pictures in C and D. What differences can you see?

E ▶ Listen to the first half of the story. What did you hear?

1	Which person says they're getting wet?	Sue	Robert	Michael	Vicky
2	Who is frightened about something?	Sue	Robert	Michael	Vicky
3	Which person is getting cold?	Sue	Robert	Michael	Vicky
4	Whose house can the friends go to?	Sue's	Robert's	Michael's	Vicky's

F ▶ Which picture comes next?

G Look at the last picture and tell the end of the story.

14 'Are you hungry? Thirsty?'

A **What am I? Find the answers in the word wheels.**

1 A clever insect called a bee makes me!
2 Add me to water to make a really cold drink!
3 I'm made of sugar and fruit. Put me on your bread!
4 There's milk in me and you eat me with a spoon! I'm sweet!
5 I'm white and I look like sand but don't put me in your tea or coffee!

B **Read and guess what I'm making – pasta, sandwiches or fries?**

1 You can make this at home with eggs and flour, but I bought a bag of this from a shop. Put it carefully into very hot water and cook it for between five and nine minutes.

....

2 To make cold ones, put food like salad, eggs or jam between two pieces of bread. Some people like making hot ones with cheese or meat inside.

....

Complete the sentences about the other food.

3 To make these, you need .... , which you .... into thin pieces and .... People eat them with food like .... and ....

....

C ▶ Listen and tick (✔) the box.

1 What can Betty have for dinner?

A ☐   B ☐   C ☐

2 What did David have for lunch?

A ☐   B ☐   C ☐

3 What does Katy want for breakfast?

A ☐   B ☐   C ☐

4 What did Tony eat at the party?

A ☐   B ☐   C ☐

D Read the sentences and write one word on each line.

How often do you ...	never	sometimes	every day	points
1 .....do..... sport?	a	b	c	....
2 eat different .... of fruit and vegetables?	a	b	c	....
3 go .... bed very late?	a	b	c	....
4 have drinks with sugar .... them?	a	b	c	....
5 eat chocolate and sweets?	a	b	c	....
6 eat foods .... burgers, chips or sausages?	a	b	c	....
7 walk up or .... stairs when you could use a lift?	a	b	c	....
8 drink four or more glasses .... water each day?	a	b	c	....
9 forget to .... breakfast?	a	b	c	....
10 play on the computer for more .... two hours each day?	a	b	c	....

E Now answer the questions. Draw a circle round a, b or c.

15 'What's for dinner?'

A ▶ Listen and draw lines.

Paul   Anna   William   Richard

Jill   Harry   Vicky   May

B Read the text. Choose the right words and write them on the lines.

Swans

		in	of	on
Example	Swans are the largest water birds ....in........ the world. You often see wild swans on lakes or rivers. Most swans are white,			
1	but you can .... see black swans in some countries.	also	next	too
2	Swans look lovely but be careful if one .... really near to you. If a swan	comes	coming	came
3	suddenly .... frightened, it will try to fly away and might hurt you. Swans have really strong wings!	feel	feeling	feels
4	Their necks are .... than any other birds' necks because they use them to help find	longest	longer	long
5	food in the water. In a river .... are lots of plants and insects for swans to eat!	here	then	there
6	Swans live together in pairs or families. Young swans don't usually leave their parents .... the next new babies join the family.	during	before	by
7	Some swans don't like cold winters so when it starts getting colder, ... wonderful	this	all	these
8	birds begin the long journey .... warmer environments.	on	to	at
9	Wild swans usually live for about twenty years but swans .... live in places like	which	what	who
10	zoos .... live for fifty years!	can	would	must

C Find out what Grace and Tom are doing!

D ▶ **Listen and order the pictures 1–6.**

WILLIAM'S WONDERFUL —Honey Cake!—

YOU NEED:

EGGS ○   HONEY ○

FLOUR ○   MILK ○

SUGAR ○   BUTTER ○

LEMON ○

E Write funny food sentences for all your friends!

Mary ate all of Mum's meat at midnight on Monday!
Tom had too many tomatoes at ten o'clock on Tuesday!
William had some wonderful watermelon on Wednesday!
Tony took tea to his thirsty teacher at teatime on Thursday!
Fred had fish fingers and fries at five o'clock on Friday!

Sue ....

Sally ....

F Ask and answer questions.

Let's talk about food. What's your favourite food?

Who cooks most of the food in your home?

Tell me about the food you ate for dinner yesterday.

Where do you eat at home?

16 'Let's have a picnic!'

A Write what you can see.
Add one word to each sentence.

Example: This is often made of metal.
You use it to cut meat.

..........*a knife*..........

1 Most people put their food on a round .... before they eat it.
2 I'd love a .... of lemonade. Can I open that new bottle?
3 If you want to have some soup, put it in a ....
4 Only put a little black .... on your food because it tastes hot!
5 Does your family buy milk or juice in a .... ? Mine does.
6 You can use a metal .... to mix different kinds of food together.
7 Dad adds a little ...., not pepper, to meat when he cooks it .
8 I know someone who prefers using .... to eat rice.

B Look at the pictures and tell the story.

1

2

3

4

C **Look at the picture and read the story.**
Write words to complete the sentences. Use 1, 2, 3 or 4 words.

That is such a good idea!

Lucy West likes being a secretary, but when it's hot and sunny she looks out of the window at the view and dreams of holidays in the countryside. Last Thursday morning, the weather was wonderful. But there was so much work to do. Lucy turned on her computer and started answering lots of important emails.

At twelve o'clock she said to Sue, the other secretary in the room, 'We need a holiday! But we can't leave the office. What shall we do?'

'Let's have a holiday here in our lunch break!' Sue said. 'Turn off the computers!'

The two women moved their desks and computers and put a blanket from the office cupboard in the middle of the floor. Sue fetched two glasses and a cold bottle of lemonade from the office kitchen and put a box of cookies from her bag on a big white plate. Sue played a CD of wild birds singing and the warm light from the sun came through the open office window.

The women sat on the blanket, had their picnic, closed their eyes and dreamed of being in the countryside. It was difficult to start work again that afternoon! When Lucy got home her husband asked, 'Did you have a busy day?' 'Yes! I wrote 148 emails,' she laughed. 'But I went on holiday too!'

Examples

Lucy likes her job. She's a .... *secretary* ....

Lucy looks out of the window when it's .... *hot and sunny* .... outside.

Questions

1 Last week, the .... was very good on Thursday.

2 Lucy had to write lots of .... that morning.

3 Another secretary called .... worked in the office too.

4 At twelve o'clock, Sue and Lucy .... their computers.

5 Sue went to the office kitchen to get a .... and some glasses.

6 The women listened to .... of some birds singing.

7 When Lucy arrived home she said to ...., 'I wrote 148 emails but I went on holiday too!'

D **Let's play a guessing game!**

17 'A day's work'

A Look at the pictures. Write the jobs.

Crossword grid:
- 1 m _ _ _ _ _ _
- 2 c _ _ _ _ _
- 3 p _ _ _ _ _ _ _
- 4 j _ _ _ _ _ _ _ _
- 5 s _ _ _ _ _ _ _
- 6 d _ _ _ _ _
- 7 (down)

B Read the sentences. Write the jobs from the crossword.

1 <u>a photographer</u> I take pictures of interesting places and people for magazines.

2 .... I find out about things that happen and then write about them for newspapers and different television channels.

3 .... This person works in an office, answers the phone and writes messages, emails and letters.

4 .... I work in a restaurant. I cook for people who come to have meals.

5 .... You go to see these people if you are ill. They look at you, give you medicine and make sure you get better.

6 .... This person can repair your car if you have a problem with it.

7 .... People come to sit and watch us on a theatre stage. They can also see us in some TV programmes.

C ▶ Listen and write the numbers of the job in A.

a ....   b ....   c ....   d ....

D Which job in A do you like best? Which is the worst? Write the jobs next to the numbers.

1 is the worst job! 7 is the best job!

1 ....   2 ....   3 ....   4 ....

5 ....   6 ....   7 ....

E ▶ What did Sarah take to each place?
Listen and write a letter in each box.

letters [B]

a map [ ]

a scarf [ ]

an umbrella [ ]

a jacket [ ]

a camera [ ]

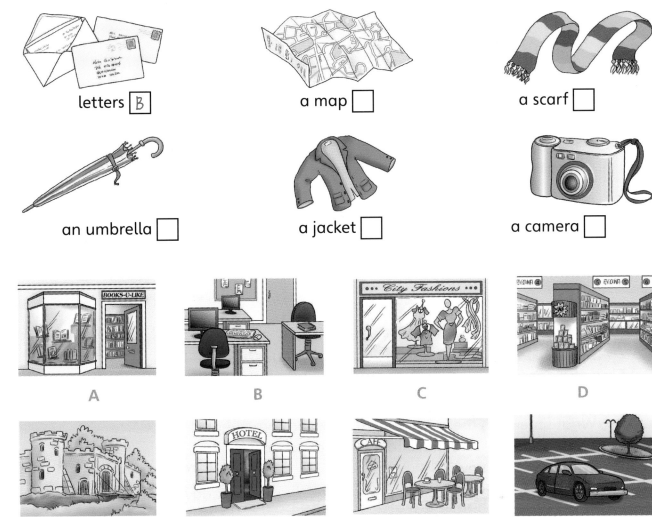

A

B

C

D

E

F

G

H

F Look at the pictures and tell the story.

1

2

5

THE NEWS

OUR JOURNALIST SARAH TALKS TO JOHN CLOCK

3

4

18 'Time and work'

A What's the time?

a  1

....3 o'clock....

b ☐

....

c  ☐

....

d  ☐

....

e ☐

....

f  ☐

....

B ▶ Listen to the conversations and read questions 1–4.
Find the correct answers in A. Write 2, 3 and 4 in the boxes in A.

1   What time is lunch today?
2   What time does the boy's television programme begin?
3   What time does Ann have to get up for school?
4   What time is it now?

C Read the story. Choose a word from the box.
Write the correct word next to the numbers 1–5.

Michael is in London. He flew there last week with some school friends. They're having English lessons at a college in the city centre. He's talking and sending messages to the other people in his ......family...... on the internet. He does this in his afternoon lesson break.

His father, Jim, teaches (1)...................... but he's at home now. His mother, Mary, is a businesswoman. She's visiting a (2)...................... in China where they make phones and watches. His sister, Emma, is in another country too. She's (3)...................... with her class in the mountains!

Michael's family had to think carefully about a good time to talk to each other because the time is different in each of the four countries. Michael can (4)...................... the computer room in London at 4 pm. Back at home, his dad turns on the computer at 7 pm to talk. After a day in the mountains, Emma goes online in her hotel at 5 pm. But their conversation is much (5)...................... for Michael's mother. Where she is, it's 1 am!

> Example
> family   spending   later   Art   hour   factory   fast   skiing   fetch   use

Now choose the best name for this story. Tick (✔) one box.

Emma's funny day at the airport ☐

Michael's family conversation ☐

A lesson for Michael's dad ☐

D ▶ **Listen and tick (✔) the box.**

Example What's Kim's job?

A ✔   B ☐   C ☐

1 How does Kim go to work?

A ☐   B ☐   C ☐

2 What time does Kim start work?

A ☐   B ☐   C ☐

3 Where does Kim have lunch?

A ☐   B ☐   C ☐

4 What was Kim's first job?

A ☐   B ☐   C ☐

5 What does Kim like most about her job?

A ☐   B ☐   C ☐

E Play the game! Which job have I drawn?

19 ‘Answer my questions’

A Read the story. Choose a word from the box.
Write the correct word next to numbers 1–5.

Daisy Brown had a little brother called David who made her angry! David was only five but he never, never stopped asking questions! 'How does a ......*light*...... turn on and off, Daisy? How long is a dinosaur's tail, Aunt Sally? Why can dogs' ears (1) .... some noises that I can't, Grandpa?'

He sometimes asked really difficult questions. 'What's in the middle of our planet, Mum? Why have tigers got (2) .... bodies, Daisy?' People usually said, 'I don't know, David!'

One day, Dad, Daisy and David were (3) .... in the town centre when David pointed to the new science museum and asked, 'What's inside that (4) ...., Daisy?' Daisy didn't know, but their father did. He smiled. 'It's a museum. We might find lots of answers to your questions there.'

Daisy (5) .... going to museums. She turned to David and said, 'Let's go there now! What shall we find out about first?' That was a difficult question for David. 'I don't know!' he said!

> **Example**
> light   candy   hear   deciding   end   building   loved   striped   half   shopping

Now choose the best name for the story. Tick one box.

Our family's favourite animals ☐

Answers for David ☐

Dad's visit to town ☐

B ▶ Listen and colour the museum picture in A.

C Write the correct question words after numbers 1–12. Ask your friends the questions!

> How many   How much   How often   How old   What
> What time   When   ~~Where~~   Which   Who   Whose   Why   How

	Your name ....
Name	Example ....*Where*....... do you live?
....	1 .... is your surname?
....	2 .... is the cleverest student in this class?
....	3 .... did you come to school today? By bus?
....	4 .... birthday is in April?
....	5 .... are you? 10? 11?
....	6 .... did you get up this morning? Seven o'clock?
....	7 .... homework do you have every day? Too much?
....	8 .... people live in your house? Four? Five?
....	9 .... is the best place to go? A museum or a shopping centre?
....	10 .... do you listen to music? Every day?
....	11 .... will you go home? Soon?
....	12 .... are you learning English?

D Write questions! Answer questions!

on the beach

in class

in a museum

at a party

1 .... ?

2 .... ?

3 .... ?

4 .... ?

E Play the game! Questions mingle.

43

20 'Calling and sending'

A What has Charlie lost?

B Read the story. Choose words from the phone. Write the correct words next to numbers 1–5.

When Charlie got back home after his school trip to Hardhill Castle, he put everything that was in his backpack on the hall table. He suddenly began to feel really worried! 'Where's my phone?' he said. 'I was .... sure .... I had it with me. Oh no! It's (1) ....!'

'What am I going to do?' he asked himself. 'I can't (2) .... Holly and speak to her. She'll be angry because I forgot to phone her yesterday. I can't go (3) .... and read my emails. And Mrs Hope, our history teacher, told us to look at that (4) .... to find more information about sea journeys in the nineteenth century. There's also that new game that Michael told me about. It's so exciting! I wanted to play it this evening.'

And then he thought: 'What's that noise? It (5) .... like my phone! So where is it? Oh! It's in my trouser pocket!' Charlie took it out, looked at the screen to see who was calling him and said, 'Hello Holly!'

sounds

instrument

~~sure~~ call

ONLINE

strange

repeats

advice

MISSING

WEBSITE

Choose words to make the best name for the story.

Holly	changes		finds		headteacher.
Charlie	turns on	then	sends	his	rucksack.
Mrs Hope	loses		repairs	her	phone.

C **When did these things happen? Write years.**

1 Martin Cooper had the first mobile phone conversation.

....

2 Shops sold the first mobile with an address book, email and calendar.

....

3 You could only save 30 phone numbers on your phone.

....

4 First phone with a camera.

....

5 British engineer Neil Papworth sent the first SMS (text message).

....

6 The first phone with internet.

....

7 You could pay for things in shops with your phone.

....

8 The first phone with a game.

....

1973   1983   1992   1993   1994   1998   1999   2000   2011

In ....

D **Ask and answer questions about Katy and George's phones.**

Katy's new phone	
When/get	?
Colour	?
Big/small screen	?
Who/often call?	?
Where/keep	?

E **Play the game! The verb–noun chain.**

'The time of the year'

A How many words can you find on the calendar page?

September						
1 fall	2	3 a week	4 hours	5	6	7 midnight
8	9 summer	10	11 a weekend	12	13	14 a year
15	16 midday	17 days	18	19	20 a century	21
22 months	23	24	25 minutes	26	27 a diary	28 winter
29	30					

Write the blue words on the line:

shortest time > minutes, ...
.... > longest time

B Choose words from the calendar in A and write them on the lines.

Example There are usually 365 days in this.	a year
1 In some parts of the world, this means 'autumn'.	....
2 The weather at this time of the year is the warmest.	....
3 This is another way of saying 12.00 in the afternoon.	....
4 In each hour, there are 60 of these.	....
5 Most people are awake for about 16 of these each day.	....
6 This is another way to say Saturday and Sunday.	....
7 You can see the names of 12 of these on any calendar.	....
8 A new one of these begins every hundred years.	....
9 This is usually the coldest and darkest time of the year.	....
10 This is when one day finishes and another begins.	....

C Put the words in the spring, summer, autumn or winter boxes.

baby animals   making a snowman   making a sandcastle
on the beach   leaves falling   camping   starting school   cold   wet
finishing school   flies   flowers   hot   skiing   warm   picnics   soup
bears   sleeping   January   April   December   July   August   February
March   June   September   May   November   October

| spring | .... |
| | .... |

| summer | .... |
| | .... |

| autumn (fall) | .... |
| | .... |

| winter | cold .... |
| | .... |

D Look at the pictures. What differences can you see?

A

B

E Read the message and write the missing words.
Write one word on each line.

Example Uncle George is great! This afternoon, he drove me ......_to_......

1 Appletree Forest where I met two .... my friends,

2 Harry and Sarah. They .... their bikes there today.

First, we made boats from an old newspaper and then sailed

3 .... best one down the river. It moved fast because

4 it .... quite windy today. We were lucky! We caught four fish!

5 Uncle George .... a fire from some wood so we could cook

the fish for our lunch.

We all had a really wonderful time.

F Play time games!

22 'Important numbers'

A How long / tall / high / far away? Match the drawings and numbers.

384,403 km

32 cm

8 m

1.70 m

2,616 m

B Tick (✔) the pictures of the people you read about.

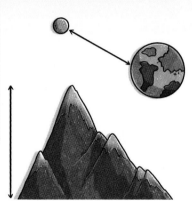

The youngest and the oldest

Here are some interesting facts. Did you

Example .... _know_ .... that the youngest driver in

1 the world passed his test 27
March 1974 when he was 14 years 235 days
old!

The youngest golfer to hit a golf ball all

2 the way to the flag .... called
Matthew Draper. Matthew hit the ball 112

3 metres .... he was only 5 years

4 212 days old when he .... that!

Sydney Ling was only 13 when he wrote,

5 .... also filmed, the famous
movie, 'Lex the Wonderdog', in 1973. The

6 film was 92 minutes ....!

Harry Stevens was the oldest person in the
world to get married when he became a new

7 husband at the age ....103!

8 .... new wife was already 84!

The oldest person to fly in a plane was
Charlotte Hughes. Her 110th birthday
present was a passenger ticket to fly

9 .... London to New York but
actually, that wasn't the last time she

10 .... in a plane! She travelled
by air again when she was 115! What a
wonderful adventure!

C **Choose the right words and write them on the lines in B.**

Example know   knew   knowing
1 in   on   at   6 long   longer longest
2 be   were   was   7 with   by   of
3 but   or   if   8 Her   Your   His
4 doing   does   did   9 from   off   for
5 because and   after   10 flies   flew   flying

D ▶ **Listen and write.**

Tamae Watanabe

1 Climbed: ....
2 Age the first time: ....
3 Date of second time: May ...., 2012
4 Time they got to the top: .... a.m.
5 Mountain is: .... metres high

E **Complete the sentences with your numbers!**

I'm .... metres tall.

My lucky number is ....

My birthday is on ....

My telephone number is ....

I think I know .... English words!

I often travel on the number .... bus.

It takes me .... minutes to come to school.

My school is .... kilometres from my house.

About .... people live in the village/town/city where my home is.

And today, I am ☐ years ☐ months and ☐ days old!

F **Do the birthday puzzle!**

PROJECT

23 'World, weather, work'

A Look and read. Write yes or no.

Examples

The person who's holding the yellow phone is looking at its screen. ....yes...........

The children are wearing the same school uniform. ....no..............

Questions

1 The woman with pink gloves is walking through the entrance. ....

2 Several pieces of paper have fallen out of the man's bag. ....

3 It's easy to see that the weather is very foggy. ....

4 There's a picture of an astronaut between the office windows. ....

5 Someone has already arrived and turned on a computer. ....

6 The building's double doors are both bright blue. ....

7 A man who's wearing striped trousers is falling over. ....

B Add information to Mr Wild's business email! You choose!

Good morning, Dan!

Thanks for your message. Actually, I've got an engineers' ..meeting.. at 9.30 and after that I need to add some important information about our (1) ....
to the website, but I can meet you at (2) .... Is that OK with you? Come to my (3) .... I want to hear all about your trip to the (4) ....
factory! I also want to show you the photos of the (5) .... that we're going to put in the (6) .... next month. Please bring the (7) ....
to our meeting. I want to look at those, too.

I've got to collect some (8) .... tickets in the lunch break so I'm sorry I can't join you for lunch! Enjoy your (9) .... ! It always tastes so good!

I had problems with my car this morning so had to get a (10) .... into town. I think it's going to (11) .... later so can you give me a lift home this afternoon? I live in Middle Street which is very near the (12) ....

I've got to hurry to the meeting now.

See you later, Richard Wild

C **Look and read. Choose the correct words and write them on the lines.**

the internet   a photographer   a desert

ice

a storm

	Businessmen and women go to this place to work and have meetings.	*an office*
1	When you are online, you can find all kinds of information on these.	....
2	This person takes the pictures that you see in newspapers or magazines.	....
3	If you visit this very dark place in the rocks, you might see bats inside it.	....
4	You might feel frightened in this loud, wet and windy kind of weather.	....
5	Important people, like kings or queens, lived in this kind of building in the past.	....
6	In this kind of weather, it's very difficult to see places that are far away.	....
7	Only plants that don't need lots of water can grow in this hot, dry place.	....
8	You look at words and pictures on this part of a computer when you're studying.	....
9	Look up when you are outside in the day or at night and you will always see this.	....
10	You should be good at writing emails, messages and letters on a computer in this job.	....

fog

a castle

a cave

a hill

the sky

a screen

a secretary   websites   an office

D **Two words or one word?**

there's ...   I've ...   who's ...   we're ...

E **Play the game. The verb–noun chain!**

PROJECT

24 'Leaving and arriving'

A Choose two words to complete each sentence.

station path love countries ride sky visit ~~pilot~~ catch planets
passenger city wheels ticket journey astronauts airport ~~fly~~

Example A ......*pilot*...... sometimes uses a helicopter to ....*fly*........ to
people who are in danger or need someone to help them very quickly.

1 You have to wait at a railway .... if you want to ....
a train.

2 Sometimes .... travel into space in rockets to find out more about
science and other ....

3 A .... has to pay a taxi driver quite a lot of money to take them
from one part of the .... to another.

4 When you go for a .... on a bicycle, you use your feet to make
its .... turn round and round!

5 In many .... you need to buy a .... before you can
travel on a bus or train.

6 People need to get on a plane at an .... to go on a long
.... by air.

7 People who .... adventures might go for rides in hot air balloons
high up in the ....!

B ▶ Listen to the sentences about picture 1. How is picture 2 different?

1

2

Example   In my picture, the man on the motorbike has got a red bag.

C Draw lines between words that mean the same.

1 **Travelling** to London takes three hours.
2 Mum **drove me** to the city centre.
3 Grandma **took** the wrong bus!
4 I **rode my** bike to school last week.
5 We **crossed** the desert **on foot**.
6 We **arrived at** the airport at six thirty.
7 My parents **flew** to the holiday island.

A gave me a lift
B caught
C walked across
D went by helicopter
E trips
F The journey
G went by
H got to

D ▶ How did Uncle Bill get to each place?
Listen and write a letter (A–H) in each box.

A   B

C   D

E   F

G   H

E Answer Peter's questions about Uncle Bill. What does Jane say?
Write 1, 2, 3 or 4 words.

1 Peter: Why did your uncle go to the airport?
   Jane: He went there to meet ..*an important person*.. .

2 Peter: What's the quickest way to get to the museum?
   Jane: Going to the museum .... is the quickest.

3 Peter: Where did your uncle lose his money?
   Jane: He dropped it in the .... when he was riding there on his bike.

4 Peter: Did your uncle enjoy his ride in the helicopter?
   Jane: Of course he did! It was .... because he was so high in the air.

5 Peter: Did your uncle go to any places which weren't for work?
   Jane: Yes. On Tuesday, he went to a restaurant which is next to
   a .... I love the pizzas there. They're great!

25 'What shall we do next?'

A Read about Ann and Pat in the museum.

Ann and Pat are on their school trip. They're in a really interesting computer science museum. They're sitting at a large table where there are three computers and lots of other things to look at. Ann and Pat are playing a science game on two of the computers. Their teacher is watching them. Ann and Pat aren't alone. Quite a lot of other children are in the same part of the museum. They're looking at something on the wall.

Imagine a picture of Ann and Pat in the museum and answer the questions.

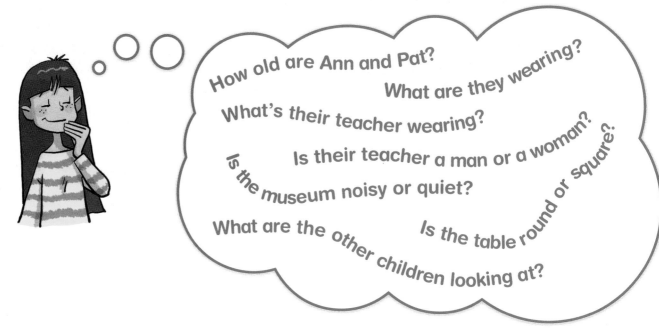

How old are Ann and Pat?

What are they wearing?

What's their teacher wearing?

Is their teacher a man or a woman?

Is the museum noisy or quiet?

Is the table round or square?

What are the other children looking at?

B Ask and answer questions about two school trips.

C ▶ Listen and write ten things to take on a trip.

D Listen and write yes or no.

1 ...yes...   2 ....
3 ....   4 ....
5 ....   6 ....
7 ....   8 ....

E Look at the picture and read the story.

Mary's naughty friend

Mary was too excited to eat her dinner. She suddenly jumped up from the table and said, 'I'm going to phone Grandma before I go on my school trip!'

Mary's grandmother was surprised to hear her granddaughter on the phone. 'It's quite late, Mary.' 'I know, but I'm so excited,' Mary answered. 'I'm going to go on a school camping holiday. My friends and I are going to have lots of fun!' 'Wow!' her grandmother said.

'We have to take pens and write about birds we see,' Mary said. 'But my friend and I are going to look for a big, dark cave with wild bats and furry mountain monsters inside! We don't get frightened by things like that!'

'I know. You're very brave,' Grandma laughed. 'What else?' 'Well, we have to take things for washing,' Mary answered. 'But my friend and I are going to wash outside. We can clean our dirty faces in the rain! And we have to take things for eating, like forks and spoons, but my friend and I are going to put sweets and chocolate biscuits in our rucksacks too, so we can have midnight snacks. And we're going to put an ugly plastic spider in Nick White's bed!'

'Who's this naughty friend of yours, Mary?' Grandma asked. 'I'm not going to tell you that, Grandma,' Mary answered. 'It's a secret!'

F Write some words to complete the sentences. You can use 1, 2, 3 or 4 words.

Examples   Mary couldn't ....*eat her dinner*.... because she was too excited. She left the
table and went to phone her ....*grandma*....... .

Questions

1   Mary's grandma was .... when Mary phoned her.

2   Mary and her friends are going to have fun on their ....

3   Mary and her friend want to find wild bats and .... in the cave.

4   Grandma thinks Mary and her friend are ....

5   Mary says. 'We're going to wash .... in the rain!'

6   Mary and her friend are going to eat .... in the night.

7   Mary doesn't say the name of her friend because that's a ....

G Play the game. Topic words!

26 'Where can we go on holiday?'

A Match four of the word circles with the pictures.

camping
tentcampingtorch
rucksackclimbing
sailing
island view
city hotel entrance
rewild animals jungle adventure

B Complete the holiday diary. Write one word in each space.

I spent most ....of....... this morning in the pool but in (1) .... afternoon, Dad drove us to a city (2) .... was quite far away. I thought that (3) .... quite boring. After dinner, we (4) .... down in a circle round a fire and told stories. One was (5) .... a person who lived in the mountains and met a wild bear! We went to bed really late. Sleeping (6) .... the ground isn't easy! It's quite cold (7) .... hard. But camping is much more fun than staying (8) .... a hotel!

C Read the conversation and choose the best answer (A–H).

Example

Ben: This is our last week of school before the holidays!

Helen: .....C.....

1 Ben: Where do you usually go?
Helen: ....

2 Ben: Do you stay in a hotel?
Helen: ....

3 Ben: So, you have to take lots of things with you, then!
Helen: ....

4 Ben: What do you do during the day?
Helen: ....

5 Ben: This year, we're going to go to London. Have you been there?
Helen: ....

A No. A science tour two years ago.
B What a big building!
C Yes, it's great, isn't it! We're going to go away. Example
D We love looking for wild animals!
E Of course, like blankets and torches.
F No, in a tent. We prefer doing that.
G To the mountains like you did last year.
H No! You're so lucky! Can I come too?

D Look at the pictures and tell the story.

1

2

3

4

5

E Listen and colour and write and draw.

27 'It's the holidays! Bye!'

A Make a story with the seven pictures.

B Read the story. Choose a word from the box.
Write the correct word next to the numbers 1–5.

Every summer, Jim goes to the ....beach........ with his parents and two cousins, Emma and Sarah. One afternoon they all sailed to a little island. They took a
(1) .... with them and ate it on the rocks there.

Then Emma said to Jim and Sarah, 'Let's go for a walk round the island by ourselves. We might find something really exciting here!' They did! They found a big dark
(2) .... where the sea water went in and out. 'Perhaps a horrible wild animal with frightening eyes lives in here!' Jim whispered. Emma laughed. 'Or perhaps pirates come and (3) .... their gold and silver treasure here!' she said. The children spent a long time (4) .... shells from between the rocks there. When they were getting ready to leave, they saw a man who was standing in the entrance. 'Oh no! It's a pirate!' Sarah said.

'Don't worry! It's me!' Jim's dad called. 'Wow! What a (5) .... place! But come on! It's time to go home!'

> **Example**
>
> beach   map   wonderful   missing   hide   picnic   lost   collecting   cave

Now choose the best name for the story. Tick (✔) one box.

Our sailing game   ☐

Fun on the island   ☐

The pirate family   ☐

58

C ▶ **Listen! What's Lily going to do today? Tick (✔) the boxes.**

play chess ☐   eat lots of biscuits ☐

watch a TV programme ☐   go on a journey ☐

repair her bicycle ☐   write messages ☐

join a club ☐

play video games ☐   be really lazy! ☐

read an adventure story ☐

D **Decide what you are going to do tomorrow!**
Complete the sentences.

Tomorrow is the first day of my holidays!
I'm not going to get up until ....
I'm going to have .... for breakfast.
Then I'm going to put on my .... and
call my friend whose name is .... because
....
After lunch I'm going to going to ....
Then I'm going to go to .... and then I'm going
to ....
After having my favourite dinner which is .... ,
I'm going to ....
And I'm not going to go to bed until .... !
See you!
Bye for now. 😊

E **Play the game. Really?**

59

28 'I want to win!'

A What was each person doing? Read and write names.

At twenty-five to six, who:

Example	was moving one of the chess pieces?	....
1	was feeling worried about the game?	....
2	was lifting something above people's heads?	....
3	was explaining the game to the others?	....
4	was hoping he might win soon?	....
5	was sending someone a message?	....
6	was thinking about the next meal?	....

B Listen and draw six things in picture A.

C Read Sam's text message. Write the missing words.

Hi Kim! I can't believe it! I won the adventure story competition!
I wrote ....*about*.... a boy who got lost in the rain forest. The
first ⁽¹⁾ .... is great! It's tickets for me, a friend and my
family to go to the new adventure park, the one ⁽²⁾ .... is
near Henley City. We'll go on Saturday. ⁽³⁾ .... you like
to come with us? Dad can ⁽⁴⁾ .... us all there in our car.
It's a really exciting place with ⁽⁵⁾ .... of frightening rides!
Ask your mum and then tell me at school tomorrow.
See you!
Sam

D ▶ Anna's competition. Listen and tick (✔) the box.

What kind of competition is Anna
getting ready for?

A ☐   B ☐   C ✔

1 Who is helping Anna?

A ☐   B ☐   C ☐

2 What is the date of the competition?

A ☐   B ☐   C ☐

3 How did Anna find out about the
competition?

A ☐   B ☐   C ☐

4 What is the first prize?

A ☐   B ☐   C ☐

5 Where is Anna going to go now?

A ☐   B ☐   C ☐

E Play the word game! How many new *Flyers* words can you make?

An adventure story competition

'Doing sport! Having fun!'

A ▶ Write twelve things you can see in the picture.

snow
....

....

B ▶ Listen and draw lines.

Vicky   Ben   Jim   Tom

Alex   Emma   Jill

C Write answers.

Which girl is Jill? Where is she? How old is she? What is she wearing?
What is she doing? How is she feeling? Is she having fun?

....

....

....

D **Write the answers to the sports quiz.**

1   When people do this sport, they stand or sit and try to catch something that lives in the water. They might eat it later!   ....

2   Five players bounce and throw the ball in this sport. Teams wear special shorts and T-shirts in different colours.   ....

3   You move quickly down a hill or mountain in this popular sport. You can only do it when there is snow on the ground.   ....

4   You can try to win alone or with your partner in this sport. You use a round bat to hit a small ball across a table.   ....

5   When we do this sport, we use our arms and legs to push our bodies through the water.   ....

6   In this sport, you hit a very small hard ball across grass. There are usually 18 flags in the place where you play it.   ....

7   People do this sport on ice. It looks like dancing sometimes!   ....

8   When we play this, we hit the ball in the air with our hands or arms. We don't want the ball to fall on the ground!   ....

9   Sometimes people race in boats in this sport. It is usually a safe sport but might be quite dangerous if the wind is strong.   ....

10   In this sport, players hit a hard ball across the grass or across ice. The team that scores the most goals are the winners!   ....

E **Look at the pictures in B and E. What differences can you see?**

F **Listen and write your answers.**

30 'Summer and winter sports'

A **Which person won the bike race?**

The person who won wore red gloves …

… and forgot their sunglasses …

… and their bike had black stripes on it.

… and shorts without pockets …

… and their wheels looked quite unusual …

B **Write to, because or so.**

1 Holly and I went to the mountains .....*because*..... we love snow sports.

2 Holly can't ski .... she took her sledge.

3 We took our skates too .... there was ice on the lake.

4 After lunch, Holly and I picked up some snow .... make a snowman.

5 Our hands got really cold .... we put on our gloves.

6 I laughed at Holly .... she fell over in the snow.

7 Holly was angry with me .... she threw snowballs at me!

8 After that, I put on my skis .... ski down the mountain.

C **Read the story and write answers. You can use 1, 2, 3 or 4 words.**

The wrong suitcase!

Lucy and her parents, Mr and Mrs Field, put their summer clothes and swimming and sailing things in their big, brown suitcase and drove to the airport. Lucy was excited because she was going on a sports holiday. When they got to the airport, Lucy's dad showed their tickets and then the family hurried to the bookshop to choose some magazines.

After that, they went to get on the plane. Lucy's seat was by the window! During the journey, Lucy's mum read about a famous ice hockey team, her dad talked to another passenger about a golf match and Lucy watched an adventure film about mountain climbing. When they got off the plane, they took a taxi to the hotel. 'Wow!' said Lucy when they arrived. 'Look at all the sailing boats! And, look! You can play table tennis by the pool. Oh! Can we go swimming? I can't wait until tomorrow!'

'Not yet, Lucy,' her mother said. 'We have to take our things up to our room first.' When Lucy's father picked up the suitcase, he said, 'That's strange. This feels much heavier than it did before!'

Mrs Field laughed. 'You think that because you're tired after our long journey! Come on! I've got our key. Look! Our room number is 501. It's on the fifth floor.' They went up in the lift, found their room and went inside. Then Lucy's dad opened the suitcase to take out their swimming things. 'Oh no!' he said. 'Whose ski hat is this? Why are there three pairs of gloves and all these warm socks in the suitcase?'

What a terrible mistake! The family had the wrong suitcase!

Examples

The Field family put all their holiday things in a ̲b̲i̲g̲,̲ ̲b̲r̲o̲w̲n̲ ̲s̲u̲i̲t̲c̲a̲s̲e̲ .

Lucy was feeling really ....̲e̲x̲c̲i̲t̲e̲d̲............ about going on a sports holiday.

Questions

1   Before they got on the plane, the family bought .... from a shop.

2   On the plane, Lucy's mum read about some famous .... players and her father talked about golf.

3   The adventure film that Lucy saw was about ....

4   Lucy wanted to .... when they arrived at the hotel.

5   They went up in the lift because their room was on .... floor.

6   .... opened the suitcase to get out the swimming things.

7   Inside the suitcase, they found a hat, ... and some warm socks!

D **Look at the pictures and tell the story.**

E **Play the game. Why?**

31 'Here and there'

A What are these? Find them in the picture in C and say where they are.

1
2
3
4
5

B Find these people in C. Answer the questions about each person.

1
2
3
4
5

1 How old is this person? Guess!
2 What kind of hair has she/he got?
3 What is she/he doing?
4 What is she/he wearing?

C Look at picture a and read. Write yes or no.

a

Examples		
	All the people are sitting down.	.....yes.....
	One of the children is playing with a robot.	.....no.....

Questions

1 Most of the people who are outside the café are young children. ....
2 There are enough green chairs for everyone to sit on. ....
3 All the tables you can see are round and the same colour. ....
4 The blue bicycle that's next to the café has fallen over. ....
5 More than one person is wearing trousers with white stripes on them. ....
6 One of the grown ups is using a pen to write a letter. ....
7 Several people are hurrying past this popular café. ....

D How is picture b different?

Example

In picture **a**, a woman's wearing a green jacket.

In picture **b**, the woman *isn't* wearing a green jacket.

She's wearing a *yellow* jacket.

E Read the conversation and choose the best answer.
Write a letter (A–H) for each answer. You do not need to use all the letters.

Katy is talking to her dad, Bill, about the letter she's writing to Richard.

Example Bill: Why are you writing to Richard, Katy?

      Katy: ......D......

Questions

1 Bill: Is Richard at home?   Katy: ....

2 Bill: Where's he staying?   Katy: ....

3 Bill: What does he do in the afternoons? Katy: ....

4 Bill: When is he going to come back? Do you Katy: ....
    know?

5 Bill: Would you like to do something like Katy: ....
    that?

A Yes. It was about ten days ago, I think.

B Perhaps! Ask me again next year.

C He often visits a museum or something like that.

D Because he's my best friend. Example

E No, he's gone to London to study English.

F So do I. You can have lots of fun there!

G At the end of next week.

H With an English family who live in the city centre.

32 'Where?'

A Write the places under the pictures.

A

....

B

....

C

....

D

....

E

....

F

....

G

....

H

....

B ▶ Where did Jack take each thing? Listen and write a letter (A–H) in each box.

B

☐

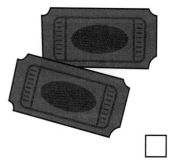
☐

☐

☐

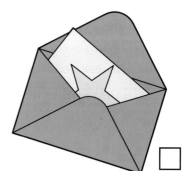
☐

C Read the text. Choose the right words and write them on the lines.

Buildings

since	for	ago

Example Thousands of years .... *ago* ...., people didn't stay in the same place because they

1 had to travel .... find food. They

2 lived in caves or slept in tents .... were made from animal fur. They cooked their food on fires that also kept them warm

3 .... the long, cold and wet winters.

4 Fires kept people safe too .... wild animals are afraid of fire.

5 Our homes .... changed a lot! Most people now live in warm, dry and safe buildings.

In some big cities you can find new buildings

6 that might have more .... a hundred floors. These are called skyscrapers.

Some skyscrapers have gardens on

7 .... roofs. You can make a 'green roof' by planting different kinds

8 .... grass there. On some city buildings, you can also see 'green walls'.

9 In big cities, ... green roofs and walls is a really good idea. The leaves on the plants help clean the air and make our

10 environment much ....

1	for	to	with
2	which	what	who
3	during	past	until
4	so	because	before
5	have	are	do
6	when	than	if
7	theirs	its	their
8	off	from	of
9	making	made	makes
10	better	good	best

D Look and describe. What is unusual about these homes?

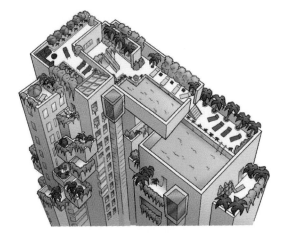

33 'At the hospital'

A Read the sentences and find the answers in the box.

Example   When you have one of these, you might have a cough and your nose goes red!

1   Someone will drive you really quickly to this place if you are suddenly very ill.

2   You go to see this person if one of your teeth breaks or hurts badly.

3   If you feel ill, the doctor might give you some of this to help you feel better.

4   You can buy something here to make a headache stop. You might also find other things like soap or combs in this kind of shop.

5   These people look after anyone who has to stay in hospital because they are ill.

6   This is often white with a blue light on its roof and you can travel quickly to hospital in it.

a	h	o	s	p	i	t	a	l	t	a
t	e	m	p	e	r	a	t	u	r	e
p	a	c	h	e	m	i	s	t	s	m
a	n	a	m	b	u	l	a	n	c	e
n	r	f	e	r	c	l	c	h	r	d
u	u	g	a	o	k	m	o	u	y	i
r	q	v	w	k	y	o	l	r	b	c
s	i	j	x	e	b	z	d	t	d	i
e	a	d	e	n	t	i	s	t	i	n
s	t	o	m	a	c	h	a	c	h	e

B ▶ Listen and draw lines.

Michael

John

Katy

William

Betty

Sarah

Mary

C Complete the sentences with names and other words from the box in A.

1   ...., the girl in the striped T-shirt, has got a .... leg.

2   ...., the boy in the white shorts, has .... his arm.

3   ...., the boy in the red jacket, has got a ....

4   ...., the girl in the purple trousers, might have a ....

5   ...., the little girl in the white T-shirt, has begun to ....

D **Read the conversation and choose the best answer.**

Example
Doctor King: Good morning, William. I'm Doctor King. What's the matter?
William: ....H..................

1   Doctor King: When did you start to feel ill?
    William: ....

2   Doctor King: Tell me what you ate yesterday evening.
    William: ....

3   Doctor King: Did the nurse take your temperature?
    William: ....

4   Doctor King: Great! Take this medicine twice a day until you feel better.
    William: ....

5   Doctor King: No, but make sure you lie down at home and remember!
                   No more than one piece of cake in future!
    William: ....

A   Four pieces of pizza and three big pieces of birthday cake.
B   It really hurt when I woke up this morning.
C   I promise I'll do that. I don't want to feel like this again!
D   Lots of my school friends came to my house.
E   That's right. She told me it was normal.
F   I started going to school when I was five years old.
G   OK. Does it taste nice?
H   I've got a terrible stomach ache.

E **Ask and answer questions about Doctor King and Mrs Ring's jobs.**

Job?	Doctor
When/work?	every night
Name/hospital?	Sky hospital
Where/hospital?	Station Road
New/old?	new

Job?	Ambulance driver
When/work?	each weekend
Name/hospital?	Swan hospital
Where/hospital?	Park Square
New/old?	old

34 ‘John stays in hospital’

A Look at the picture and read the story.

Last December, it snowed a lot. One Saturday, when John and a group of friends were playing with a sledge on a hill near their homes, John suddenly fell and broke his leg. It hurt a lot! His friends were really worried and one of them ran quickly to tell John's parents. An ambulance soon arrived to take John to hospital.

Poor John had to stay in hospital. The nurses and the other children there were friendly and kind so, at first, John didn't mind. He didn't have to go to school or do lots of homework and exams like his friends did! He just listened to music, played chess and other games on his phone and watched his favourite football team scoring lots of goals on TV. But when the Christmas holidays started, John began to feel quite bored and a little unhappy.

But then Peter Windows, a member of John's favourite football team came into his hospital room! He was carrying a Christmas tree and a bag that was full of exciting presents. And he wasn't alone! John's best friends followed Peter into the room.

John began to feel much happier and very lucky! He was really surprised when his headteacher arrived, too! He also brought John a wonderful present – some Maths and Art homework! 'Make sure you do it all before you come back to school, John!' he laughed.

Write some words to complete the sentences about the story.
You can use 1, 2, 3 or 4 words.

Examples   It was snowing last .... *December* ....
             John hurt his leg when he was sledging on .... *a hill* .... with his friends.

Questions

1   John travelled to hospital in ....
2   John liked the nurses and children there because they were so

    ....

3   John had his phone in hospital, so he could play .... on it.
4   But John felt .... and sad when the Christmas
    holidays began.
5   Then a footballer called ...., who was in John's favourite
    team, came to visit him.
6   The footballer brought John lots of .... and a Christmas tree!
7   On the same day, John's headteacher came and gave him some
    .... to do!

B  **Listen to the story. Draw lines under the differences.**

C **Read and write the missing words. Write one word on each line.**

<table>
<tr><td></td><td colspan="2" align="center">Friday</td></tr>
<tr><td>Example</td><td>I didn't have <u>   *to*   </u> go to school again today because I'm still here in hospital. But I have</td></tr>
<tr><td>1</td><td>made lots .... new friends and the nurses make us all laugh.</td></tr>
<tr><td>2</td><td>At about half .... four, the nicest nurse came into my room and turned</td></tr>
<tr><td>3</td><td>......................... the TV because the football match was starting. Our team won, two goals to one!</td></tr>
<tr><td>4</td><td>Dinner was OK too. We .... fish and chips! And Mum brought me a great present. It's the new soccer game. I played</td></tr>
<tr><td>5</td><td>......................... all evening.</td></tr>
</table>

D  **Listen and write.**

<table>
<tr><td>Example</td><td>Give John:</td><td>his <u> *art* </u> book</td></tr>
<tr><td></td><td>**Tell him**</td><td></td></tr>
<tr><td>1</td><td>Class is learning about 20th century:</td><td>.......................</td></tr>
<tr><td>2</td><td>Read page number:</td><td>.......................</td></tr>
<tr><td>3</td><td>Artist's surname:</td><td>.......................</td></tr>
<tr><td>4</td><td>Colour of answer book:</td><td>.......................</td></tr>
<tr><td>5</td><td>Day of exam:</td><td>.......................</td></tr>
</table>

E **Play the game! Put words together.**

35 'What's it made of?'

A What's this? Write the words on the lines.

Example
We use this to make small things like keys and big things like bridges
because it's very strong. .... metal ....

1 This comes from trees. It's hard but you can cut it and make
things like shelves or bookcases with it.
....

2 This comes from animals like sheep. Warm clothes like scarves
and sweaters are made with it.
....

3 You can write or draw on pieces of this. It's usually made from
trees and is flat and often white.
....

4 Expensive rings, necklaces and crowns are sometimes made of this.
....

5 You can see through this so we use it to make things like windows,
but did you know it's made from sand?
....

B What can you see?

C Put them in the boxes!

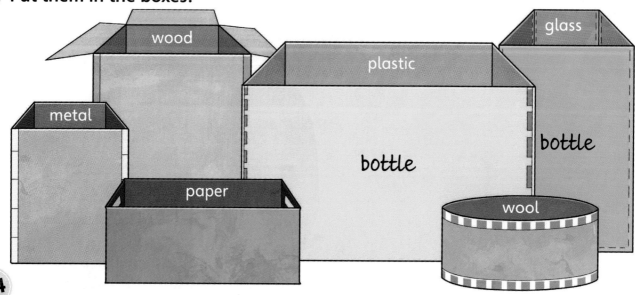

74

D William's and Sam's secret things. What are they made of? Tell me!

E  Listen and colour and write and draw.

F Read about glass. Choose the right words and write them on the lines.

Glass isn't new. People were making glass bowls and bottles more ...._than_.... 5,000

1 years ...., actually. But no one has ever found out who made glass first, or

2 when and where that ....

3 One story tells .... that some men from a ship arrived on a beach and decided

4 to make a meal. They made a fire on the sand and .... some small rocks in

5 the middle of the fire to cook on. The fire burned .... a very long time and

6 the rocks got really hot. Little pieces of rock began .... with the sand to make glass!

7 So .... next time you look through a window, look at a mirror

8 .... are holding a glass of water, think, 'Wow! This glass is made from very, very hot sand!'

Example	then	than	when
1	ago	after	already
2	happen	happens	happened
3	them	us	him
4	put	puts	putting

5	from	for	off
6	mixed	mixing	mix
7	the	a	any
8	or	because	if

G Play the game! Find things in this room.

36

'Silver, plastic, glass, gold'

A Read the clues and write the missing video game words.

Hi Peter. Here's how you play ....

Open the first door. (1) .... the tree to find the silver key. Carry the key carefully back down the tree and put it in the plastic bag which you'll find in the metal box. Carry the key and the bag up the stairs. Take out the key and use it to open the (2) .... door. Leave the key in the door and and go back down the stairs. Don't (3) .... to take the plastic bag with you.

Put the plastic bag in the tree. Now find the special rock. It's between the two lizards. Pick this up and put the rock in the metal box. Carry the box up the stairs and go through the open second door and use the rock to (4) .... the glass door. Put the box and the rock down and jump carefully through this third door. Turn on the light. In front of you is another box. This one is made of wood. The gold ring is (5) .... it. Pick the box up, run down the other stairs and throw the box on the fire. The wood will burn and then the fire will stop. You'll see the gold ring! But a monster will try to stop you picking it up. Run (6) .... back upstairs, fetch the special rock, run downstairs again and give it to the monster. The monster will go back into cave and then you can take the gold ring!

1 means 'go up' using your hands, arms and legs (5 letters)
2 not the first, not the third, the one between the two (6 letters)
3 the opposite of 'remember' (6 letters)
4 the past of this is 'broke' (5 letters)
5 means 'in' (6 letters)
6 the opposite of 'slowly' (7 letters)

B Look at pictures 1 and 2. Find six differences.
1

2

C Say what has happened in picture 2. Complete the sentences.

With the silver key, the player .... *has opened* .... the second door.

1 The player .... the glass door.
2 Someone .... on the light.
3 The player .... the box that's made of wood on the fire.
4 The monster .... back into its cave.
5 The player .... the gold ring!

D Find and write Ben's correct answers.

Vicky: It's a good game, but I think it's for younger children.
Ben: 1 ....
Vicky: How long did it take you to get the gold ring?
Ben: 2 ....
Vicky: Which part of the game did you enjoy the most?
Ben: 3 ....
Vicky: Shall we play it one more time?
Ben: 4 ....

If you want, or we could play my game.   But you aren't old enough.
I don't know. I didn't look at my watch.   No, that's the third one.
When the player broke the door!   Well, I enjoyed it and I'm ten.
I took it all the way to the fire.   It's quicker actually.
That happens in the middle of the game.   No, I'm younger than that.

E What must the second player do?

PROJECT

37

Exciting days!

A Make sentences about the things police officers do. Use the words in the box.

centre
advice
trousers
problems
stolen
exciting
jacket
car
lost
city
police
uniform
blue
police officer
things
information
station
traffic
job
dangerous
visitors
helps

B Read the text and write the missing words. Write one word on each line.

Example	David is 44. He's ...._a_........ policeman and works at the
1	police station which is one of .... highest buildings in the city centre. Every morning, he gets up at six o'clock and
2	.... on his uniform. He has to wear blue trousers, a special jacket and a blue hat.
3	When he arrives at work, he asks for information .... anything that has happened during the night. After that, he
4	jumps into his police car. Every day .... different. He might stop traffic problems at the shopping centre or give
5	advice to vistors. He tries to catch people .... have stolen things. It's an exciting but dangerous job.

C Choose a job and complete the boxes.

Name: ....

What/job?	....
When/get up?	....
What/wear?	....
Where/work?	....
Age?	....

Name: ....

What/job?	....
When/get up?	....
What/wear?	....
Where/work?	....
Age?	....

D ▶ **An afternoon at the fire station. Listen to Jim.**
Write numbers 1–4 in the boxes next to the pictures.

This is me coming down from the fire station to the .... inside a large kind of slide that's made of .... I can't stop .... !

These are some of the .... in the fire station. We're wearing fireman hats – my teacher has put one on too! And look! I'm .... in some boots and in a fireman's .... ! I love it – but it's too big for me!

Now we're getting really .... because we're playing with the water from the .... !

This is Miss Night and our .... *class* .... We're waiting outside the .... to the fire station. The ....'s quite hot and we're all feeling really excited!

E **Complete the sentences under the pictures with words from the box.**

~~class~~ wet jacket ground entrance passenger students weather
fire work traffic laughing dressing up plastic fire engine

38 'Famous people'

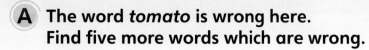

A The word *tomato* is wrong here.
Find five more words which are wrong.

1 Bill <u>tomato</u> writing adventure stories and dreams of being a famous journalist
2 like his mother one day. Last Tuesday, Bill was playing in the street with a group
3 of friends. Suddenly, a black understood with large, dark windows stopped and
4 a woman got out.

5 Bill looked at the woman and said, 'I'm classroom that's the queen!' His friends
6 didn't believe him. Then the woman came and asked Bill, 'Is there a good
7 mechanic near here?' 'There's one just round the yellow,' answered Bill. 'Could
8 you take us there?' asked the woman.

9 Bill took them to the mechanic. 'Excuse me', he said, 'but aren't you the queen?'
10 The woman trousers, 'Yes, and thank you very much for helping us.' The
11 mechanic took a photo of Bill with the queen and a week later, a downstairs
12 from the queen arrived. Bill used it with the photo to write a story for the
13 town newspaper.

B Where do these words go in the story?

likes   **letter**   **smiled**   **corner**   **car**   **sure**

Choose the best name for the story. Tick (✔) one box.

An important person visits our town ☐

Bill asks a mechanic to repair his car ☐

A trip to the concert with the queen ☐

C Write 1, 2, 3 or 4 words to complete each sentence.

Example   Bill's mum is .... *a famous journalist* ....

1 The windows of the car that stopped near Bill were large and

....

2 When Bill said. 'I'm sure that's the queen!', his friends

.... him.

3 The queen wanted to know where she could find ....

4 The queen thanked the mechanic for .... them.

5 Someone took a picture of .... that day.

6 A week later, the postman brought Bill .... from the queen.

7 Bill wrote a story for .... about the day the queen visited
the town.

D Read the queen's diary. Write one word on each line.

Example
1

Earlier today I went to ....visit........ a new museum that was about 100 kilometres away. My driver .... me there in the car.

2

On the way home, the car started making strange noises, so we decided .... find a mechanic quickly.

3
4

We saw a .... in the street with some friends and he knew a mechanic .... worked just round the corner.

5

Tomorrow morning, I'll send him a letter to thank him .... helping us!

E ▶ Look at the pictures and listen. Tell the story.

1

2

3

4

5

F Write your answers to these questions.

1 Which famous person would you like to meet? ....
2 Why is this person famous? ....
3 Why do you like this person so much? ....
4 What does this person look like? ....
5 Would you like to be famous one day? ....

81

39 'In villages and towns'

A You're walking through a village. What can you see?

B Read the story. Choose a word from the box. Write the correct word next to numbers 1–5.

Mrs Forest works in the village post office. No one knows if she's 75, 85 or 95, but she's very old. The post office is the most popular place in the village. It's always ....*full*....... of people, so Mrs Forest can ask lots of questions.

Daisy Cage came in to buy six ⁽¹⁾ .... 'What was your camping holiday like, Daisy?' Mrs Forest asked. 'What an adventure! Did you like sleeping in a ⁽²⁾ .... ?'

Pat Down needed some brown paper. 'Hi, Pat!'' Mrs Forest said. 'You've ⁽³⁾ .... your motorbike, haven't you? What will you buy with all that money?'

It was Mrs Forest's birthday last Saturday. Her husband came into the post office and gave his wife a big red balloon. 'How lovely!' she said. Then Mr Forest took a ⁽⁴⁾ .... pizza out of his bag. Would you like this or something else for your birthday ⁽⁵⁾ .... ?' Mr Forest liked asking lots of questions too! 'Chocolate cake, David!' Mrs Forest answered with a big smile.

> Example
> full   dinner   large   tent   leave   thanks   stamps   excited   score   sold

Now choose the best name for the story. Tick (✔) one box.

Mrs Forest makes a pizza! ☐   More and more questions! ☐

Pat's special birthday present! ☐

C ▶ What did Lucy's mum buy in each place? Listen and write a letter in each box.

a   b   c   d   e   f   g   h

D Find words in each wheel. What are the three places in town?

E What's this? Choose the correct words and write them on the lines.

a restaurant   a flashlight   a journey   an entrance

Example	You can sit here and eat a meal that a cook has made for you.	...a restaurant...
1	People make things like computers or phones or fridges in this kind of place.	....
2	This has two wheels and you can ride it from one place to another in the town or countryside.	....
3	Two people can sit on this to move quickly down a hill but there must be snow on the ground!	....
4	When you go to this, you can hear music and watch people playing instruments on a stage.	....
5	This is all the cars, trucks, lorries and motorbikes we can see on a busy road.	....
6	If you remember to take this with you, you can turn it on and see better in dark places.	....
7	When you go from the street to the inside of a building, this is what you walk through.	....
8	People who enjoy doing this like sleeping in a tent more than in a hotel room.	....
9	Footballers in each team are always trying to score these during the match!	....
10	This describes the time we take and the way we travel from one place to another.	....

goals   traffic   a seat

a sledge   offices   railway   a factory

a concert   camping   a bicycle   snowboarding

F Play the game! Guess the describing word.

83

40 'What a strange planet!'

A **What's unusual about the animals in this picture?**

B **Look and read. Write yes or no.**

Examples   Most of these strange animals have tails. ....yes.......

There are more than five pink clouds in the sky. ....no..........

Questions

1   The cow with wings is in the corner of the picture. ....

2   The biggest animal in the picture looks like a large mouse. ....

3   There are several trees but they all look different. ....

4   A fat green monkey is riding down the river with a blue horse. ....

5   Something has started eating one of the bananas. ....

6   A yellow kangaroo is skipping under a tree that has orange leaves. ....

7   A pink frog that has spots on its body and really long legs is flying
    above the water. ....

C ▶ **Listen and answer the questions about the competition.**

Which place would
you like to visit?

What's the most
beautiful sound that
you've ever heard?

What's the best photo of an animal
or place that you've ever seen?

D Read the story. Write some words to complete the sentences about the story. You can use 1, 2, 3 or 4 words.

Hello, my name's Tom and I live in a busy city, but last June I went camping in the countryside for the first time. I went with Grandpa Pat and my two cousins who are three years older than I am. It was exciting because we didn't arrive until midnight. It was very quiet and we couldn't see very much because it was so dark. Putting up our tent was quite difficult!

When I woke up early the next morning, there were so many unusual sounds outside. I could hear birds that were singing all kinds of different songs. I could also hear some water outside, but it sounded much noisier than a river. I opened up the tent quietly because I didn't want to wake my grandfather and cousins and stood up slowly to see where we were. 'This is the most beautiful place that I've ever seen!' I thought. 'I can't wait to walk up those hills and through those woods.'

Then, between some high trees, I saw the lovely waterfall and all the rocks below it. It was only a little way away from our tent. 'What a beautiful view and that's such a wonderful sound,' I whispered to myself. 'I wish I could see and hear this every morning!'

Examples

Tom went camping last June with his grandfather and his ......*two cousins*......

Tom was ..*three years younger*.. than his cousins.

Questions

1   It was already dark when they put up the tent because they arrived at
    ....

2   Tom could hear lots of wonderful sounds when he woke up the
    ....

3   One of the sounds came from something that was louder ....

4   Tom didn't want to wake the others up so he quietly .... and
    went outside.

5   Tom thought the hills and woods looked more .... than any
    other place he knew.

6   Not far from their tent, Tom could see some rocks below a ....

7   The water was making .... that Tom wished he could hear it
    and see this view every morning.

E Write yes or no.

Meet the pirate actors

A Write the correct words on the green lines and the correct names on the pink lines.

1   In the film, ... *William* ...... is never lazy. He looks after the ship's flags and tidies the kitchen. He's wearing swimming ...... *shorts* ...... with red stars on them.

2   William's grandfather, whose name is .... spends lots of time fishing. He has dressed up in an old red and white striped T-shirt. One of his legs is .... of wood! He thinks he's the best actor in the film!

3   William's sister's name is .... She's got a noisy pet parrot and she .... wears shoes in the film! Can you see her toes?

4   .... is William's grandmother. She does the cooking on the ship and has to sing a lot in the film. Part of her costume is a pair of striped ....

5   William's father, ..., is busy all day. He counts his money, watches the sea for .... sharks and tells everyone what they must do! But he sometimes forgets what he has to say in the film!

6   William's mother never takes her spotted hat or silver necklace off. She sails the ship at night in the bright .... of the moon. Her name is ....

shorts   air   tights   made   never   light   wheel   pushes   wished   dangerous

B ▶ **Listen and colour and write and draw.**

C **Look and read. Write yes or no.**

Examples   Only one child is swimming in the sea in this part of the film   .....yes.....
            The sky above the sea is full of clouds.   .....no.....

Questions
1   More than one cameraman is filming William in the water.   ....
2   One of the fish has stripes on the middle of its body.   ....
3   The larger shell is nearer to the treasure than the smaller one.   ....
4   You can see all of the shoe that is in front of the treasure box.   ....
5   The girl in the boat is wearing a T-shirt that has spots on it.   ....
6   A little comb has fallen from one of William's pockets.   ....
7   There is a lot of money on the sand in front of the open box.   ....

D **What was each person doing when the photographer took these photos?**

> hiding behind a pyramid   holding a sweet puppy   eating some special pasta
> collecting lovely shells   climbing a rock   riding a friendly camel

E **Think hard! How much can you remember?**

87

42 Holiday news

A ▶ **What has Mary already done? Tick (✔) the boxes.**

B **Read the email that Mary is going to send to her family.**

Dear Mum and Dad,

I'm sorry that I haven't written to you earlier, but don't worry. I'm fine and we're having a great time. This is only a short email because I've got to hurry. We're going to visit the pyramids today! I hope you like this picture of us in the desert! I'll send you some more photos soon. Betty took a good one of me in the entrance to our hotel and another of us all in the pool.

See you on Saturday. Our plane will arrive at about three o'clock so I'll get my backpack and meet you at the passenger exit at about a quarter to four.

Lots of love, Mary

C ▶ **Look at Mary's photo. Listen and draw lines.**

Harry   Sarah   Kim

Katy   Betty   Alex   Michael

D Look at Mary's other photo. What differences can you see?

E Read the postcard and write the missing words.
Write one word on each line.

Dear Nick,

We've already been here ....for....... *four days! There*

Example

1 .... *so many things to see here! We've already visited*

2 *a museum* .... *had gold toys and strange clothes in it.*

We've been to the theatre too. I understood the actors because

3 *they* .... *in English. The story was about a famous queen*

4 .... *lived 4,000 years ago.*

5 *I have* .... *go now. This evening, our headteacher is going*

6 *to take* .... *to a restaurant that's outside the city and I'd*

7 .... *to wash and dry my hair and change my clothes! See*

you next week at school.

Mary

F Make sentences about the things you've done today.

89

43 'Have you ever ...?'

A Write the words to complete the questions.

1 Have you ever ....gone.............. to a ....concert.............. ?

2 Have you ever .... in a .... ?

3 Have you ever .... with .... ?

4 Have you ever .... a .... competition?

5 Have you ever .... to .... or New York?

6 Have you ever .... a leg or an .... ?

7 Have you ever .... a famous .... ?

B Make sentences about your group.

Everyone has ....

Most of us have ....

Quite a lot of us have ....

About half of us have ....

Only a few of us have ....

No-one has ....

C Read about winter sports. Choose the right words and write them on the lines.

Winter sports

Example	Have you .... *ever* .... skied down a mountain? Skiing is an exciting sport but it isn't a new one.	yet	before	ever
1	.... are several old paintings on rock	We	There	They
2	walls inside caves that show people	what	who	whose
3	are skiing. Some of .... cave paintings are more than 5,000 years old!	these	this	that
4	About 180 years ago, on a small farm in the mountains, Sondre Norheim's father .... wood from the forest to make his young son a pair	use	used	using
5	.... skis. Sondre loved putting on his skis, jumping off the roofs in his village and skiing	by	with	of
6	down the hills. .... he grew up, Sondre made the first skis that could turn on soft snow and	How	Why	When
7	won .... important skiing competitions.	one	many	another
8	People still .... Sondre 'the Father of Skiing'.	call	calls	calling
9	Now, both skiing and snowboarding are really popular sports! Lucky families can stay in wonderful mountain villages where ski lifts take .... to the top of the mountain so they can ski	them	him	their
10	.... snowboard back down again! What fun!	if	because	or

D ▶ Look at the mountain picture in Unit 29. Listen and write yes or no.

1 ....   2 ....   3 ....   4 ....

5 ....   6 ....   7 ....   8 ....

E Let's talk about things we've all done!

44 `What has just happened?`

A **Read the two party invitations.**

Hi!
Please come to my party on Saturday, 12 December at the Concert Café.
It starts at 5 pm.
Choose between pizza or burgers!
Make sure you wear sports shoes because we'll play football later!
Love, Emma

To: Betty; Richard; Helen; Fred; Robert; Tom
From: Pat
Subject: My birthday party

Hello everyone!
This year, my party's at my house – 28 Museum Street – on 15 November. Add it to your calendar. It starts at 4.30pm.
We'll have Mum's chocolate cake!
We'll play lots of different games. Dress up in your funniest clothes!

Write about the parties in these boxes.

Emma's birthday party

Date?	12 December
Time/start?	
Place?	
What/eat?	
What/wear?	

Pat's birthday party

Date?	15 November
Time/start?	
Place?	
What/eat?	
What/wear?	

B **Read the conversation and choose the best answer (A–H).**

Example Jill: It's your birthday today, isn't it, Pat?
        Pat: ......F...... .

1 Jill: Are you going to have a party?
   Pat: ....
2 Jill: Have you invited all your friends?
   Pat: ....
3 Jill: And what time does it start?
   Pat: ....
4 Jill: Oh! Has your mum bought a lot of food?
   Pat: ....
5 Jill: Great. Have a good time!
   Pat: ....
   Jill: And next time, please invite me too!

A	At five, I think. I'm not sure.
B	Yes, we've just got some.
C	Yes, she's here today.
D	Happy birthday!
E	Thank you. I will!
F	That's right. I'm twelve. *Example* How did you know?
G	Yes. I'm really excited.
H	Only about ten of them.

C Look at the picture in D.
   Try to find something for each letter of the alphabet.

   Examples   a ....armchair....   b ....bookcase....

D ▶ Listen and draw lines.

Betty   Richard   Helen   Fred

Robert   Tom   Pat

E Read Pat's diary and write the missing words.
   Write one word on each line.

TUESDAY 15 NOVEMBER

Example   I was twelve .....years..... old today. I got some
1   excellent presents! Ten .... my friends came
   to my party. Tom gave me a computer game called
2   'Bats in your basement!' I haven't tried to ....
   it yet, but it looks good. Sally bought me a T–shirt.
3   .... 's got an alien on the front! I got a new
4   keyboard from Mum and Dad. But .... most
   exciting present was from Uncle David. He's just given
   me a sweet little puppy with long, soft, gold-coloured
5   fur! I'm going to .... it 'Honey', I think!

F Play the game! Find your partner.

45 Talking about the time

A Look at the boxes, read the sentences and write or colour.

.... ☐	.... ☐	March ☐	.... ☐
May ☐	June ☐	.... ☐	.... ☐
September ☐	October ☐	November ☐	.... ☐

1. Write the names of the six missing months on the lines.
2. How long is each month? Write the number of days in the small boxes.
3. Write today's date in the correct month box.
4. Write your birthday in the correct month box.
5. Colour the summer months bright yellow and the spring months bright green.
6. Choose colours for the autumn and winter months. Another way of saying 'in the autumn' is 'in the ....'.
7. Draw a star in your favourite month on the calendar.

B ▶ Listen and tick (✔) the box.

Which place did Richard and his class visit this year?

A ☐ B ☐ C ✔

1. When did Richard's school holiday begin?

APRIL 29 JUNE 4 SEPTEMBER 18

A ☐ B ☐ C ☐

2. What did Richard do on holiday?

A ☐ B ☐ C ☐

3. What did Richard bring home?

A ☐ B ☐ C ☐

4. When can Richard's aunt watch the holiday film?

A ☐ B ☐ C ☐

5. What will Richard wear?

A ☐ B ☐ C ☐

C Read the text. Choose the right words and write them on the lines.

Time

Our planet takes 365 and a quarter days to ...... move ...... round the sun, so every four years we have a 'leap' year. In a leap year,

Example — moving   moved   move

1. .... are 366 days so we — there   those   they
2. add another day .... — to   with   over
   February. You will see this on calendars and in diaries.

3. Most months have 31 days, but four .... — from   of   with
   the months only have 30 days. February is the
4. month .... only has 28 or 29 days. — whose   which   what
5. Twice a year, ... countries in the world — many   much   lots
   decide to change the time by one hour. We do this
6. .... we want to use more light from the — because   than   but
7. sun. This helps people who .... outside. — working   works   work
   This is also better for people that have to do
8. .... lot of driving. — the   a   any

We change the time twice a year. In March, we make the time one hour later and in October, one hour earlier. So, on the first day after the clocks

9. .... changed in October, — have   has   having
10. .... can stay in bed for another hour! — he   you   it

D Look at the train timetable and answer the questions.

PROJECT

Jacktown	08:30	09:15	11:10	12:30
Fallwing	09:05	10:15	11:45	13:30
Letmore	09:55	10:55	12:35	14:20
Keepfield	10:10	11:25	12:45	14:45
Endwich	11:15	12:25	13:40	14:55

1. How many stations will my train stop at after I get on it at Jacktown and before I arrive at Keepfield? ....

2. How long is the journey to Keepfield if I leave Fallwing on the eleven forty-five train? ....

3. It's five past two. How long must I wait at Letmore station until the next train arrives? ....

4. I must arrive in Endwich by twenty past eleven. Which train must I catch from Letmore station? ....

5. I want to travel from Jacktown to Endwich on the fastest train. What time does it leave? ....

6. If I leave Jacktown station at a quarter past nine, spend an hour in Keepfield, then catch the next train to Endwich, what time will I arrive? ....

We're all at home today

A ▶ Who's talking? Match the numbers and letters.

6

5

4

3

2

1 [D]

Are you going snowboarding today?

Is John at home?

Did you repair your bicycle?

Were there lots of people at the match?

Can your Mum give me a lift into town later?

Have you seen our new puppy yet?

No, I didn't have time.

We are, but not until this afternoon.

Yes, I have. It's really sweet.

She can't today. Sorry!

He isn't now, but he will be later.

Yes, there were thousands!

F

E

D

C

B

A

B ▶ Where has Katy's mum put Katy's things? Listen and write a letter in each box.

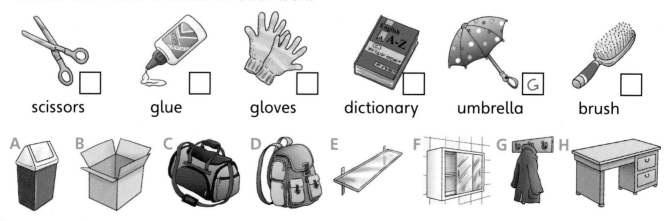

scissors　　glue　　gloves　　dictionary　　umbrella [G]　　brush

A　B　C　D　E　F　G　H

C Read the story. Write some words to complete the sentences about the story. You can use 1, 2, 3 or 4 words.

Naughty Daisy

Last Sunday, our family wanted to go to the zoo, but the weather was very cold and windy so it wasn't a good day to be outside. We decided to stay at home.

After lunch, my little sister Daisy was really bored. She came into my bedroom and asked, 'Tony, play this board game with me!' 'Sorry, Daisy,' I said, 'I can't. I have to study for my Science exam. I'll play with you a bit later.'

Daisy went into the living room. 'Will you play with me, Dad?' she asked. 'Yes, but I'm busy now,' he explained. 'I'll play with you in 20 minutes. I must finish reading this important information on your school's website first.'

Mum was talking on the phone in the hall. Daisy began asking her to come and play, but Mum said, 'Not now, Daisy. I'm explaining something to Aunt Sarah.'

'No-one wants to play with me,' thought Daisy. She was really angry. She didn't like playing all alone so she went upstairs to fetch her favourite doll.

When Dad finished his work, he called Daisy's name. Then Mum finished speaking to Aunt Sarah and called Daisy's name, too. But Daisy didn't answer. I stopped writing and ran downstairs really quickly. I could hear her laughing loudly. 'She's in the kitchen by herself,' I thought. 'What's she doing in there … ?'

Examples

The family didn't go out because it was ...*very cold and windy*... outside.

That afternoon, Daisy was feeling very ....*bored*......... .

1   .... was studying for his Science exam.

2   Daisy's father was reading some .... on the internet.

3   Daisy's mum couldn't play because she was speaking to ....

4   Because she didn't want to be alone, Daisy went upstairs to find ....

5   When Daisy's mum stopped talking on the phone and ...., she didn't answer.

6   Tony stopped what he was doing and .... when he heard Daisy laughing.

7   Tony didn't know what Daisy was doing in the ....!

D Play the game!

Can I come too / to / two?

47 'I will or perhaps I won't'

A ▶ **Listen. What might Sam be one day?**

1   Sam won't be a .... *dentist* .... because he thinks that's a .... *boring* .... job.
2   Sam might be an ambulance .... but that's a .... job.
3   Sam may be a .... because he thinks that's an .... job.
4   Sam says he will be a .... That's a really .... job!

B **What are these children thinking? What about you?**

I .... be a ....

I .... be a ....

I .... be a ....

I .... be a ....

C **Choose your answers. Tick (✔) the boxes.**

In ten years …

1   I'll be
☐ at school.
☐ at university.
☐ at work.

3   I won't have
☐ any homework.
☐ any friends.
☐ any money.
☐ any problems.

5   I may have
☐ a castle.
☐ a motorbike.
☐ a pool.
☐ a horse.
☐ an island.
☐ a violin.

2   I'll live
☐ here.
☐ in another city.
☐ in another country.
☐ on another planet.

4   I'll be
☐ single.
☐ married.

6   I might be
☐ a businessman/woman.
☐ a doctor.
☐ an engineer.
☐ a nurse.
☐ a farmer.
☐ a sports star!

D ▶ **What will Mrs Kind give to each of her friends?**
Listen and write a letter (A–H) in each box.

Grace [B]
George [ ]
Alex [ ]
Michael [ ]
Sarah [ ]
Robert [ ]

A   B   C   D
E   F   G   H

E **Answer me!**

Yes, I will.
I may!
I might.
No, I won't.

Will you travel to other parts of the world in space rockets in the future? ....

Do you think you will you travel to the moon one day? ....

Do you think you will have a conversation with an alien one day? ....

Do you think you will have to live on other planets in the future? ....

F **What will happen?**

48 Doing different things

A Write each word next to *man, woman, man or woman.*

wife **king** **partner**

grown-up **queen**

husband

man   ....

woman   ....

man or woman   ....

B Read about this actor. Choose a word from the box. Write the correct word next to numbers 1–5.

Hi! Many of you may think I'm ....*called*........ Sue Pepper but that's just the name I use for work. My name's Kim Short, actually! I'm 21 and an actor. I've already been in several (1) .... but now I'm working with my best friend, Holly, on a new TV programme. You can see it soon on Channel 12.

You'll see that I often get frightened because I have to go on unusual adventures like (2) .... with sharks or jumping off high rocks into a (3) .... My adventures are usually quite safe but some of them look really dangerous!

We were filming the programme in a place that's a long way away last week so someone had to fly me there in a helicopter every morning which was fun. I felt really (4) .... !

When we aren't filming, I like spending some quieter (5) .... at home on our farm. My husband and I love horse-riding in the hills there.

> **Example**
> called   time   far   tasting   future   important
>   walking   waterfall   movies   swimming

Choose the best name for Sarah's story. Tick (✔) one box.

Kim, the actor ☐   Holly's new helicopter ☐   Sue's wild horse ☐

C **Read the note and complete Kim's speech bubbles. Write 1, 2, 3 or 4 words.**

We can't film the walk on Monday next week, Kim, so you'll do the hot air balloon ride that day. You'll have an unusual train journey on Friday – more information about that later. The walk with wild animals (the one you wanted to do on Monday) will be on Thursday now. Sorry! And on Tuesday, you won't go sledging in the mountains. You'll have a rock climbing lesson. We've made sure you'll enjoy Wednesday. You'll spend that snowboarding.

George

On Wednesday, I'm going to go ....

And I'm doing the .... on Thursday now.

Monday will be exciting. I'm going up in a .... !

It's the .... on Tuesday.

But I'm going to go on .... on Friday.

D ▶ **Listen and write.**

Nick Silkwood visits our town

Example	Nick's son's name:	*Michael*
1	Son's address:	23, ... Street
	Nick	
2	Number of grandsons:	....
3	Age he started singing:	....
4	Instrument he plays best:	....
5	Song he likes most:	My ....

E **Ask and answer questions about Jack and Lily.**

F **Tell me about another person!**

49 'Busy families'

A Look and read. Write yes or no.

1   The children who are outside are both wearing scarves. ....
2   More than two people in this kitchen have got blonde hair. ....
3   The boy who's using some scissors is wearing a red sweater. ....
4   Someone has dropped some pieces of newspaper on the floor. ....
5   The youngest child is brushing her doll's teeth. ....
6   You can see that it's colder outside than inside this house. ....
7   It is easy to see everyone's legs and feet in this picture. ....

B ▶ Listen and draw lines.

Vicky   Sally   David   Lucy

Nick   Jane   Jack

C Find the second half of each sentence and write it on the line.

1   The girl with the long brush is helping .... *to tidy the room* ....
2   The woman is cutting some bread to ....
3   The girl with the pen is trying ....
4   Two girls in warm clothes are ....
5   The girl with the glue is trying to ....

> to do her homework   making a mistake   make more sandwiches
> repair the rocket   doing some shopping   making a snowman   <u>to tidy the room</u>

D Finish the answers with too or enough **and words in the snake.**

1 'Why don't you go outside, Vicky, and brush away the snow for me now?'
'Because it's too cold outside and my coat .... , Mum.'

2 'Why didn't you finish reading your other school book, Lucy?'
'Because the story and pictures are .... , Mum.'

3 'Why don't you dress your dolls up in some different clothes, Jane?'
'Because their hats are too old, Mum, and their dresses ....'

4 'Why can't you make that rocket a bit taller, Anna?'
'Because this newspaper's too thin, Mum, and this glue ....'

5 'Why aren't you doing your art homework now too, David?'
'Because, Mum, it's .... and this table isn't big enough.'

boringgoodnicebiginterestingdirtythickfunnydifficultprettyquietsmallnewstrongdryoldeasynoisy

E ▶ **Listen! Write the missing words.**

Mum: Wake up, wake up!
It's time to (1) .....go...... to school!

John: But I'm too tired. (2) .... back hurts. I want to
stay in (3) ....

Mum: No, John, no! You must (4) .... up now, it's late!

John: It's not. It's too early. I'm not going (5) ....!
I'm not going anywhere! There's a storm outside.
Listen! It's raining (6) .... hard and it's too
(7) ....

Mum: No, John, no! It's sunny (8) .... warm. It's a lovely
day and you're (9) .... holiday. You were having a
(10) .... dream!

F **Look at these pictures. What differences can you see?**

G **Play the game! Guess my four things.**

50 On TV

A ▶ **Listen and write.**

Example	Name:	Richard ......Hudson......
1	Job:	....
2	Makes things with:	wood and ....
3	Starts work at:	....
4	Works in his:	....
5	What making now:	....

B Ask and answer questions about Tony, Vicky, Alex and Kim.

C Peter Sun is talking to Grace. What does Peter say?
Write a letter (A–H) for each question.

Example	Peter:	......G......
	Grace:	Hello, everyone! Hello, Peter! It's great to see you again.
1	Peter:	....
	Grace:	Yes. I got here at midday.
2	Peter:	....
	Grace:	To make a new film with my husband.
3	Peter:	....
	Grace:	The life of a famous painter.
4	Peter:	....
	Grace:	Only a week. We are going to film a movie in the jungle next month.
5	Peter:	....
	Grace:	Next spring.

A Why have you come to London?
B How long will you be here?
C Have you just arrived?
D What's the film about?

E When will you finish filming that movie?
F Who are you going to visit now?
G Hello, Grace! How are you?
H Me too! I love doing that!

D **Read the text and choose words from the box for 1–5.**

Every Thursday, ...*millions*........ of people in villages, towns and cities (1) .... on their televisions at 7:30 to watch Peter Sun's wonderful programme which is on (2) .... Four.

If you enjoy learning about people who have some of the most exciting jobs in the world, you (3) .... watch it too!

Each week, Peter finds out all kinds of different information about famous (4) ...., band members, artists and exciting businessmen and women.

Tonight, Peter Sun's conversation will be with the (5) .... star, Grace Keys! Don't miss it!

> millions   should   Channel   turn   film   screen   improve   singers   gate

E **Read Sam's email to Peter Sun and answer questions.**

@

Hi Peter,
I went to the World Zoo today. Someone told me about the new dolphin trainer who works there. Her name's Alex Sugar. She's not famous like other people on your programme, but she's very interesting and funny and so are the dolphins at the zoo! But there's a problem. Alex Sugar can come to the film studio, but the dolphins can't. So we'll have to take all our cameras and lights to the zoo and film her, the dolphins and the programme there. Do you agree with that? Sam

F **Look at the pictures and tell the story.**

Peter and the dolphins.

1

2

5

3

4

51 Here's my news

A Write the parts of Low Island School you can see.

a  b  c  d  e  f

the office   ....

....

> the sports hall   the library   the computer room   ~~the office~~
> the playground   the dining room   the entrance

B ▶ Which parts of the school is Nick in? Listen and write letters from A.

Example   d   1 ....   2 ....   3 ....   4 ....

C Ask and answer about Jill and Robert's hotel website information.

Jill Kite's hotel

Hotel noisy/quiet?	noisy
How many rooms?	27
Sport?	tennis
Internet/bedroom?	yes
What/see from/balcony?	coconut trees

Robert Brown's hotel

Hotel noisy/quiet?	quiet
How many rooms?	610
Sport?	swimming
Internet/bedroom?	no
What/see from/balcony?	car factory

D **Read the two emails and the sentences in the large box. Who wrote each sentence? Anna or Fred?**

Which sentences are from Anna's email? She's studying English.
Which sentences are from Fred's email? He's at the beach.

Text 1

Dear Ben,
Here is a picture of the school where I'm studying English.
Anna

Text 2

Dear Ben,
Here is a photo of the beach which is near our hotel.
Fred

1	a	We've been here since Monday and I can see an island from my hotel room.
	b	Everyone here is very nice, but I wish I was better at speaking English!
2	a	I'm making friends which is good because sometimes we have to do homework together.
	b	I met some other children in the pool and we stayed together all afternoon.
3	a	Later today, we're going to play football in the park behind our classroom.
	b	We usually have lunch in a café that's only ten metres from the sea.
4	a	The grown-ups sit in the sun most of the day. Boring!
	b	Some of the others prefer to stay inside with the computers but I don't.
5	a	At the end of the day, the school lets us choose between sport and watching DVDs. My listening has really improved because of all the films I've seen here!
	b	In the evening, we walk down the path to the sea and sing songs round a fire. I never feel alone here!

E ▶ **Listen to Paul. He's talking about his day.**

F **Write about your school or news.**

52 'What a lot of questions!'

A Complete each question with words from the box.

> How often   What kind   How long   What   ~~Who~~
> Have you ever   How   Which   How many   Whose

Questions | Me | ....

1 ....Who.......... 's your luckiest friend?

2 .... do you go online?

3 .... have you been in this class?

4 .... times have you been on a theatre stage?

5 .... instrument do you prefer – the drums, the guitar or the violin?

6 .... scored a goal in an important match?

7 .... of holiday do you like best?

8 .... birthday in your family is it next?

9 .... tall are you now?

B ▶ Listen. Which questions from A does Holly's mum answer?

C Write your own answers, then ask a friend.

D Read the story. Write some words to complete the sentences about the story. You can use 1, 2, 3 or 4 words.

Harry and the difficult questions

Harry Doors loved learning. He had hundreds of books in his room at home and liked using his computer to find out about jungles, clouds, kangaroos or anything else that he found interesting.

One day Harry's teacher said, 'Would you like to be on a TV programme, Harry? It's a competition on Channel 7 for the cleverest children in the country. You'll have to answer several difficult questions!' Harry said, 'Yes! Of course!'

The next day, a man called Mr Silver came to Harry's school to give him some advice and important information about the competition. 'Before we can film you, Harry,' he said, 'I have three questions. Ready?' 'Yes!' Harry whispered. He was suddenly feeling a bit frightened! 'Good! Where's the River Thames?' 'In London,' Harry said quietly.

'Well done! What's 27 times 5?' '135!' Harry answered quickly.

'Great! Which is the highest mountain in the world?' 'Mount Everest and it's 8,848 metres high!' Harry answered with a big smile on his face. He knew that all his answers were right.

'Excellent!' the man said. 'You're clever enough for the competition. Next Tuesday a taxi will bring you and your parents to Television House at six o'clock! Now, I just need to know your age. When's your birthday, Harry?' Harry was so excited he couldn't speak. 'Sorry!' he said. 'I've forgotten!'

Examples

Harry's surname was ....Doors.........

In Harry's room at home there were <u>hundreds of books</u>.

Questions

1   Harry used his books and .... to find out lots of things.

2   The first person to tell Harry about the .... on Channel 7 was his teacher.

3   The .... in Harry's country will be on the TV programme.

4   The name of the man who came to see Harry was ....

5   The man gave Harry some .... about the competition.

6   Harry was happy because .... to the man's questions were right.

7   But Harry couldn't remember the date of his .... !

E Listen and colour.

53

'Finding your way'

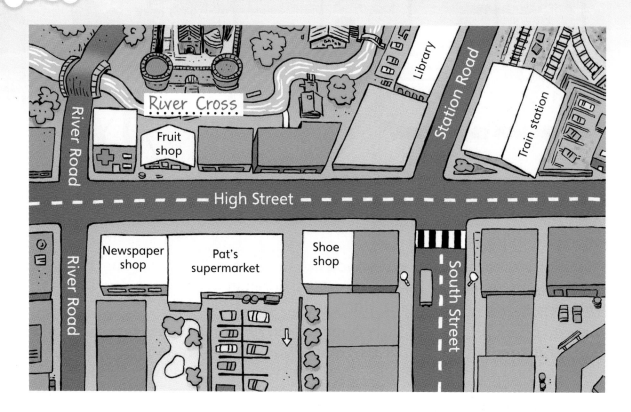

Ⓐ Look at the map and read about Castletown. Find each place.

1. During your trip here, why not stay in Station Hotel. It's across the street from the railway station and next to the library in Station Road?

2. The bank is opposite the station. Its entrance is in South Street.

3. The post office is in High Street, across the street from Pat's supermarket.

4. There's a small sports shop on River Road behind the newspaper shop in High Street. Their hockey shirts are cheap and look great!

5. If you need to buy some medicine, don't worry. There's a chemist on the corner of River Road and High Street. It's next to a fruit shop.

6. The bookshop is in the second building in South Street. It's got a very unusual green roof! The town centre bus stops are really near it.

7. Next to the post office, there's a restaurant called The Food Village. There's a path from its back door that goes down to the river.

8. You can go online in the Internet Café, on the corner of High Street and South Street.

Ⓑ ▶ Listen and tick (✔) the box.

What does Harry need?

A   B   C ✔

1. What is opposite the library now?

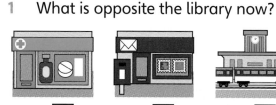

A   B C

2 Which way will Harry and his mother go to the castle?

A ☐   B ☐   C ☐

3 Which train will Harry and his mother take home?

A ☐   B ☐   C ☐

4 What will Harry have to eat?

A ☐   B ☐   C ☐

5 What has Harry lost?

A ☐   B ☐   C ☐

C Choose the correct words and write them on the lines.

a calendar   a theatre   the internet   cartoons

a city

Example	There are twelve of these in every year.	.........months.........
1	This is information we watch or read. It is about what is happening in the world.	....
2	Our homes, large shops, schools and factories are all kinds of these.	....
3	At this time of year it gets colder and leaves begin to fall from trees.	....
4	It is a good idea to walk or ride a bike on this when you are in a forest.	....
5	There are sixty of these every hour.	....
6	It is safe to cross a railway if you walk over this.	....
7	These are funny drawings that you can find in comics books.	....
8	You need to change this if you want to watch a different TV programme.	....
9	Some people put this on a wall so they can quickly see which dates to remember.	....
10	This is much larger than a town. Millions of people might live and work here.	....

autumn

months

a path

the news

minutes

a bridge   a channel   websites   midnight   buildings

D Ask and answer questions.

E Be actors in a shop or town!

PROJECT

54

'Let's have some fun!'

A **Follow the lines to make suggestions.**

Would you like   going to a basketball match?

Why don't we   playing my 'Frightening Facts' game?

Let's   draw some strange alien cartoons.

What about   to join our new music club?

Shall we   ask Dad to give us a lift into town?

How about   dress up in some funny old clothes?

We could   go snowboarding or sledging.

B **Read the conversation and choose the best answer.**
Write a letter (A–H) for each answer.

Example

Paul: Hello! Is that you, Dan?

Dan: ......B......

Questions

1   Paul: I'm feeling a bit bored.

     Dan: ....

2   Paul: We could go to the Internet Café.

     Dan: ....

3   Paul: How about seeing the new 'Bad Mix' film, then?

     Dan: ....

4   Paul: What was it like?

     Dan: ....

5   Paul: Well, I haven't got any other ideas. Have you?

     Dan: ....

     Paul: OK!

A   I've already seen that.   E   But that's such a boring place!
B   Yes, it's me! Example   F   Quite good but a bit too long.
C   So do we!   G   No, it wasn't like that.
D   Yes! Come to the park!   H   Are you? We'll let's go somewhere.

C What's happening in the theatre? Look and write yes or no.

Example

The man in the sweater has a piece of paper in his left hand. ......yes......

You can see more than two whales in the sea ......no......

1   Someone is picking up the book that has fallen behind the seat. ....

2   The girl with green wings has got really short dark hair. ....

3   On the stage, there's a boat. Its flag has got a star on it. ....

4   The person with the envelope is going up the stairs. ....

5   More than one actor is wearing a crown. ....

6   Someone has sat down on one of the seats. ....

7   The pirate is wearing a striped scarf on his head. ....

D ▶ Listen and colour and draw and write.

E Shall we write a story? Read this first!

Bill and Mary's mother had to be at the theatre on Friday. She does an important job there. Bill and Mary didn't want to go with her but they didn't want to be alone and bored at home. They thought about doing lots of different things but, in the end, they decided to climb up into the roof. Their parents kept lots of old things in big boxes there. When their mother came home, she was so surprised! Can you guess why?

55 'If I feel bored'

A Draw lines between the two halves of the sentences.

1 When I need to talk about something
2 If I'm feeling thirsty and need a drink
3 When I'm feeling really excited
4 If I'm feeling hot, I open a window or
5 When I'm ill, my mum brings me a spoon and

a I laugh a lot and sometimes sing.
b I phone my best friend.
c I get some water.
d I take my medicine.
e I turn on the fan.

B Finish these sentences about yourself.

1 When I'm tired, *I close my eyes and try to sleep for a few minutes.*
2 I laugh when ....
3 I cry if ....
4 Sometimes I feel afraid when ....
5 If I'm bored, I usually ....
6 .... make(s) me angry.
7 On days when I feel lazy, I usually ....

C ▶ Listen and say which picture. Then listen and say how picture 3 is different.

1

3

D **Read the story. Choose a word from the box.**
Write the correct word next to numbers 1–5.

Lucy and her father often go to the park together .... *early* .... in the morning. They're both going to be in a long (1) .... this summer so they try to run five kilometres. Lucy sometimes skips part of the way. She's excellent at it. She can skip faster than anyone else in her class. But last Monday, a dog (2) .... ran past Lucy and her dad when they were on the path that goes round the lake and Lucy's dad (3) .... into the water! He was really wet and very cold and had to hurry home, dry himself, find a (4) .... to put round his shoulders and sit down on the sofa.

'We can't run tomorrow, Lucy,' he said. Lucy felt unhappy when he said that because she loved running with her dad. Lucy's dad could see that Lucy was feeling sad. 'Don't (5) .... ! It will only be for one day!' he laughed. 'We can go again on Wednesday morning!'

Lucy felt much better after that!

> Example
>
> early   worry   grew   race   usually   blanket   push   suddenly   fell   problem

Now choose the best name for the story. Tick (✔) one box.

Be careful Dad! ☐   The skipping prize! ☐   Lucy's terrible cold! ☐

E **Complete the sentences about getting ready.**

Before Mr (1) .... and his daughter, Lucy, went to the park, they needed to get ready. Mr (1) .... put on a (2) .... and some (3) .... and then he fetched his sports shoes from his (4) .... and put those on, too. Lucy combed her (5) .... and put on her clean (6) .... and some (6) ....

2

4

F Tell the story.

G **Play the game! Which word?**

A **We had so much fun! Listen and draw lines.**

Robert   Lucy   Michael

Have a   holiday!

Katy   Betty   Helen   William

B Look at the pictures and tell the story.

1

2

3

4

5

C Robert's favourite word game.

gold	autumn	necklace	swim	bus
belt	camel	ski	kangaroo	minutes
red	puppy	engineer	draw	tomorrow
above	surprised	fire engine	purple	missing
taxi	black	lazy	singer	footballer
near	shorts	moustache	below	ambulance
monster	midnight	Tuesday	gloves	worried
artist	Maths	afraid	silver	monkey
hide	over	waiter	ring	message
truck	excited	kitten	dance	opposite

D ▶ **Now listen and play Betty's favourite word game!**

15   What's for dinner?

Learner A
Ask and answer questions

Grace's cake

Whose birthday?	....
What kind/cake?	....
What colour/cake?	....
Where / Grace making / cake?	....
Grace's cake large/small?	....

20   Calling and sending

Learner A
Ask and answer questions.

Katy's new phone	
When/get?	two weeks ago
Colour?	silver
Big/small screen?	big
Who/often call?	best friend
Where/keep/	in pocket

George's new phone	
When/get	?
Colour	?
Big/small screen	?
Who/often call	?
Where/keep	?

21   The time of the year

Learner A
Ask your friend these questions and write their answers.

What time of the year do you usually go on holiday?

....

Do you use a clock or a phone to wake you up for school?

....

What's your favourite month of the year? ....

Which month is usually the hottest where you live? ....

Where do you usually go at the weekend? ....

Which century would you most like to live in? ....

24   Leaving and arriving

Learner A
Ask your friend these questions and write their answers.

How do you go to school? ....

How long does it take you to get to school? ....

Have you ever been in a helicopter? ....

Would you like to go for a ride in a racing car? ....

How do you like to travel when you go on holiday?

....

15 What's for dinner?

Learner B
Ask and answer questions

Tom's cake

Whose birthday?	....
What kind/cake?	....
What colour/cake?	....
Where / Tom making / cake?	....
Tom's cake large/small?	....

20 Calling and sending

Learner B
Ask and answer questions.

Katy's new phone	
When/get	?
Colour	?
Big/small screen	?
Who/often call	?
Where/keep	?

George's new phone	
When/get?	last year
Colour?	gold
Big/small screen?	small
Who/often call?	granddaughter
Where/keep?	in kitchen

21   The time of the year

Learner B
Ask your friend these questions and write their answers.

When's your birthday? ....

How often does it rain where you live? ....

What's your favourite time of the day? ....

Which do you prefer: winter or summer? Why?

....

What's your favourite day of the week? ....

Do you prefer to tell the time with a phone, a clock or a watch?

24   Leaving and arriving

Learner B
Ask your friend these questions and write their answers.

How do you travel into town? ....

How long does it take you to get to the shops? ....

Are you afraid of flying in a plane? ....

Would you like to travel into space one day? ....

What's your favourite kind of car? ....

25   What shall we do next?

Learner A
Ask and answer questions.

Ann's school trip	
Where/now	?
Who/with	?
How/travel there	?
What/learning about	?
What/going to do next	?

George's school trip	
Where/now?	History Museum
Who/with?	favourite teacher
How/travel there?	school bus
What/learning about?	kings and queens
What/going to do next?	watch video

32   Where?

Learner A
What are these places?

1   This place is often outside a school or in a park and

....

2   ....

learn about things from the past.   ....

3   ....

you might go there if you need to catch a train.   ....

4   When you are older and finish school,

....

5   These usually have lots of bedrooms and bathrooms and

....

35   What's it made of?

Learner A
Ask and answer questions.

William's secret thing	
When/find?	last winter
Where/hide?	on top shelf in his cupboard
little/large?	large
What/secret thing?	strange key
What/made of?	gold

Sam's secret thing	
When/find	?
Where/hide	?
little/large	?
What/secret thing	?
What/made of	?

53   Finding your way

Learner A
Ask and answer questions

How do you travel to the shops?
Who usually carries the shopping?
Which shops don't you like?
Tell me about your favourite shop.

25   What shall we do next?

Learner B
Ask and answer questions.

George's school trip	
Where/now	?
How/travel there	?
What/learning about	?
What/going to do next	?
Who/with	?

Ann's school trip	
Where/now?	Science Museum
How/travel there?	train
What/learning about?	moon and stars
What/going to do next?	send text message
Who/with?	best friend

32   Where?

Learner B
What are these places?

1 ....
    people stay in them when they are away from home.   ....

2 ....
    children can swing and climb on things.   ....

3   You might go here to meet passengers who have arrived
    on a train or ....

4   Families and history teachers sometimes take children here to
    ....

5 ....
    you can go to this place to study.   ....

35   What's it made of?

Learner B
Ask and answer questions.

William's secret thing	
What/secret thing	?
Where/hide	?
What/made of	?
little/large	?
When/find	?

Sam's secret thing	
What/secret thing?	beautiful comb
Where/hide?	in a box under her bed
What/made of?	silver
little/large?	little
When/find?	last summer

53   Finding your way

Learner B
Ask and answer questions

Who goes shopping with you?
When do you go shopping?
What things do you like buying?
Tell me about your favourite shop.

48   Doing different things

Learner A
Ask and answer questions.

Jack's first job	
How old?	20
Who/work with?	older brother
What job?	fireman
How/go to work?	motorbike
Hobby?	snowboarding

Lily's first job	
How old?	?
Who/work with?	?
What job?	?
How/go to work?	?
Hobby?	?

49   Busy families

Learner A

Who makes / does your bed each day?

Who does / makes the shopping in your family?

Do you hate or enjoy doing / making spelling tests?

Are you good at doing / making different kinds of sandwiches?

Which sports can you and your friends make / do in the summer?

41   Meet the pirate actors

Learner B
What was each person doing when the photographer took these photos?

> hiding behind a pyramid   holding a sweet puppy
> eating some special pasta   collecting lovely shells
> climbing a rock   riding a friendly camel

48   Doing different things

Write one family word in each gap.

1   My .... is the person that my uncle is married to.
2   My .... are my aunt and uncle's children.
3   After your eighteenth birthday, some people think you aren't a teenager. You are a .... !
4   I can say my .... to mean 'my mother and father'.
5   I can say my .... to mean 'my grandmother and grandfather'.
6   My mum is married to my dad. She's his ....
7   My dad is married to my mum. He's her ....
8   I am a girl so I am my grandfather's ....
9   My brother and I are my grandmother's ....
10   In class we often have to work together in pairs. My .... is usually Jill.

48   Doing different things

Learner B
Ask and answer questions.

Jack's first job	
Hobby	?
What/Jack's job	?
How/go to work	?
Who/work with	?
How old/Jack	?

Lily's first job	
Hobby?	snowboarding
What/Lily's job?	photographer
How/go to work?	train
Who/work with?	uncle
How old/Lily?	18

49   Busy families . . .

Learner B

Who makes / does most of your meals at home?

What kind of job would you like to do / make one day?

How do you feel when you do / make mistakes?

Where do you usually do / make your homework?

Which is the most interesting subject that you do / make at school?

14   Are you hungry? Thirsty?

25–30

Well done! You eat very well and you look after your body. This is important because at your age you are growing.

15–24

Come on! Some of the things you do and eat are OK, but you could look after your body better.

15 or less

Oh dear! You need to eat better food and to move your body more! Fruit and vegetables are very good for you. Eat fewer snacks and less fast food. Remember to sit down when you eat meals during the day – and don't forget that breakfast is a very important meal!

Unit wordlist

1

family and friends
boy
friend
girl
people

sports and leisure
backpack
bike/bicycle
game
screen
skateboard
skateboarding
video games

clothes
clothes
coat
jeans
scarf
socks
sunglasses
sweater
trousers
T-shirts
uniform

colours
black
brown
colour
green
grey
orange
pink
red
silver
white
yellow

school
class
playground
roof
school
seat

transport
bicycle/bike
bike
lorry
road

the world around us
cloud
flower
grass
sky

other nouns
alien
bird
cow
feet
television

verbs
find
get to (school)
let's
like
play (a game)
ride (a bicycle)
say
talk about
think
wave
win

adjectives
favourite
round

prepositions
behind
by
in
on
with

expressions
Bye/Goodbye
Good morning
Good afternoon
Good evening
Hello
Hi
See you!

2

names
Harry
Helen
Mary
Michael
Peter
Robert
Sarah

people
best friend
king
people
queen
women

clothes
belt
coat
crown
dress
glove
handbag
hat
jacket
necklace
pocket
ring
rucksack
scarf
shorts
skirt
sock
suitcase
sunglasses
tights
trousers
umbrella
uniform
watch

colours
black
blue
gold
green
orange
silver

body and face
back
finger
foot/feet
hand
head
leg
neck
nose

places
castle
garden
wall

other nouns
key
letter
pen
plate
piece of paper
secret
story
table
time
top
weather
wheel

verbs
can
carry
get (wet)
go for a walk
know
listen to
look at
open
put on
rain
see
tell (someone a secret)
want
wear

adjectives
beautiful
blond(e)
clever
cold
gold
important

little
long
other
round
short
silver
small
square
thin
wet
wonderful

prepositions
over

conjunctions
if
or
so
when

3
clothes
cross
shoe
spot
square
star
stripe

colours
brown
green
purple
orange
yellow

people
man
passenger
person
woman

body and face
beard
shoulder

leisure
bag
newspaper
phone
towel

transport
boat
flag
information
screen
plane

the world around us
moon
star

time
clock
half past

verbs
clean
have got
listen to (music)
push
talk (on the phone)
take off (clothes)
write

adjectives
curly
fair
happy
large
sad
spotted
straight
striped
unhappy

prepositions
above
behind

from
next to
out
through

4
names
David
first name
Sally
surname

family and friends
anyone else
best friend
cousin
family
friend

food and drink
bread
grapes

work
singer

animals
dog
parrot
pet
rabbit

sports and leisure
club
football
guitar lesson
hobby
match
kind of music
sailing
sport
team

places
bus stop
corner

house
park
road
street

time
always
at the weekend
next week

other nouns
kind of

verbs
be called
be good at
dance
get off/on a bus
go sailing
invite someone to a party
laugh
live
look (like)
meet someone
sit
spell
steal
stop singing
tell (me about)
watch

adjectives
bright (green)
easy
excellent
favourite
funny
loud
naughty
new
same
sweet

adverbs
also
here

much
really
too

expressions
Who else?

5
animals
animal
bat
bee
bird
butterfly
camel
crocodile
dinosaur
dolphin
donkey
fish
goat
insect
kangaroo
lizard
mouse
octopus
penguin
rabbit
swan
zebra

body and face
fur
tail
tooth/teeth
wing

food and drink
carnivore
herbivore
honey
water

leisure
cartoon
film
story book

the world around us
cave
forest
lake
plant
river
rock
sea
under the ground
water

places
jungle
science museum

other nouns
group
pair (of)
part (of)
place
problem

adjectives
afraid of
dangerous
extinct
friendly
frightened
heavy
long
missing
special
strong
terrible
wild
wrong

adverbs
ago
away
only
quickly
sometimes
soon

suddenly
today

verbs
eat
feel
fly
get (colder)
grow
hop
jump
learn about
live
mean
move
swim
watch (TV)
work (hard)

conjunctions
because
but

6
animals
elephant
fly
giraffe
hippo
horse
sea animals
shark
whale

clothes
gloves
sweater
T-shirt

names
Ben
Betty

time
always
January
last birthday

last summer
last year

possessions
brush
keyboard
snowboard
thing

family
aunt
grandma
grandmother
mother
mum
uncle

leisure
camping
holiday
keyboard
violin

places
mountain
shop
zoo

other nouns
quiz

verbs
brush
buy
choose
decide
go camping
hate
love
use

adverbs
downstairs
everywhere
now
upstairs

conjunctions
because
so

7
body and face
ear
eye
mouth

the world around us
country
farm
farmer
field
hill
east
north
south
west

animals
cow
sheep
sheep dog

family
dad

food and drink
biscuit
cookie
sausages

the home
bedroom
kitchen

time
early
evening
later
morning
today

other nouns
city

truck
trees

verbs
believe
bounce
call
catch (a ball)
climb
cook
come (back)
cry
describe
do something
drive
find
follow
guess
hear
help
hold
listen
look for
lose
make someone/ something
must
pull
push
remember
run (a long way)
say
see
shout
sing
smell
speak
stop
throw
visit
watch
whisper
whistle
work

adjectives
clever
early
excited
famous
favourite
tidy
tired

adverbs
again
early
suddenly
loudly
outside
round and
round
up
very

expressions
Well done!

school
Art
artist
class
competition
computer
drawing
English
enjoy
exam
fact
Geography
History
homework
language
lesson
Maths
Music
numbers
paint
painting
partner

pencil
Science
Sport
student
study trip
subject
teacher
text
university

family
parents

places
library
pyramid
town square

other nouns
(paint) brush
us
lunch

adverbs
in the future
in the past
more than
sometimes
together
usually

verbs
add
bring
could
draw
find out
learn
look for
meet
paint
play
(instruments)
should
show
study
teach

adjectives
clean
famous
interesting
several
sure

conjunctions
but
if

expressions
Me too!
See you
tomorrow!

school
bin
book
bookcase
classroom
cupboard
desk
dictionary
eraser
glue
headteacher
pen
pencil
rubber
ruler
scissors
shelf
spelling
teacher

names
Holly
Michael

**sports and
leisure**
band
chess club
concert
volleyball

time
calendar
date
day
time
week

the home
cup
plate

materials
card
plastic
metal

other nouns
beach
bread
date
dream
leaf
map
monster
treasure

verbs
break
complete
cut
draw a circle
glue
help
forget
make sure
mean
put
repair
tick
try
understand

adjectives
difficult
easy

ready
special
thin

expressions
It's a good idea
to ...
Oh dear!
Well done!

clothes
belt
crown
pocket

animals
butterfly
cage
fur
insect
kitten

school
college
language
spelling
trip
word

the home
light
phone

other words
apple
cheese
desert
way

verbs
change
cross
fly
might
ride (an animal)
get hot
leave

adjectives
high
soft
unusual

conjunctions
if
or
when

11

**the world
around us**
desert
island
leaf
mountain
sand
shell
waterfall

places
city
town
village

**sports and
leisure**
blanket
camera
camping beds
chess game
tent
torch

verbs
be fun to do
something
camp
fall off
grow
have (a
wonderful time)
need
take (for a
walk)

walk (up)
would like to

numbers
thousands

adjectives
fun
low
other
pretty
sunny
tall
warm

conjunctions
but

adverbs
all round
at night
at the bottom
inside

expressions
Actually
Good idea!
How are you?
Is everything
OK?
What about?

12

names
Earth
Jupiter
Mars
Mercury
Saturn
Uranus
Venus

colours
dark
light

**the world
around us**
air
environment
planet
space
sun

transport
astronaut
journey
map
robot
rocket
travelling

**sports and
leisure**
badminton
golf

the home
stairs

other nouns
century
difference

numbers
degrees
twentieth

verbs
jump
look like
may
move (round)
take photos/
pictures
travel

adjectives
little
open
strange

prepositions
near
until

expressions
All right!

13

names
Alex
Emma
George
John
Sue
Vicky
William

weather
cloud
fog
ice
rain
rainbow
snow
storm
temperature
wind

**sports and
leisure**
cartoons
chess

**sports and
leisure**
ball
playground
slide
swing

family
daughter
grandpa

verbs
enjoy
fly a kite
go out
rain
snow

adjectives
cloudy
cold
dangerous
dry
fine
foggy
horrible
hot
noisy
sunny
terrible
warm
wet
windy
worse

expressions
Come on!
How about ...?
Let's
Shall we ...?

14

food and drink
apple
banana
bean
bread
burger
butter
cake
carrot
cheese
chicken
chips
chocolate
coconut
coffee
egg
flour
fries
fruit
grape
jam
juice

lemon
ice
lime
mango
meat
milk
onion
orange
pasta
pea
pear
pepper
piece
pineapple
pizza
potato
rice
salad
salt
sandwich
sausage
snack
sugar
sweets
tea
tomato
vegetable
watermelon
yoghurt

meals
breakfast
dinner
lunch

the home
glass (of water)
lift
party
stairs

names
Betty
David
Katy
Tony

work
clown

adjectives
hungry
sweet
thirsty

verbs
be made of
cook
go to bed

adverbs
carefully
late
never
sometimes

expressions
All right.
No thanks!

15
animals
bear
panda
spider

food and drink
fish fingers
picnic
teatime

time
Friday
Monday
Tuesday
Thursday
Wednesday

other nouns
bowl
baby
journey

verbs
begin
fly away

hurt
join
look (+
adjective)
mix
skip
try

adjectives
careful
lovely

adverbs
together
too many

prepositions
before
during
for (+ time)

16
food and drink
lemonade
soup
supper

the home
bottle
bowl
box
CD
chopsticks
cup
fork
glass
knife
plate
spoon

work
break
email
office
room
secretary

other nouns
view

verbs
answer (an
email)
be called
close (your
eyes)
dream
fetch
go on holiday
let's
mix
pick up
prefer
taste
turn off
turn on

adjectives
angry
busy
open

adverbs
so much
such a

prepositions
after

expressions
That's a good
idea!
Don't worry!

17
work
actor
cook
doctor
journalist
mechanic
photographer
TV star

places
bookshop
café
restaurant
stage
supermarket
theatre

**sports and
leisure**
front page
letters
magazine
message
news
skiing
stage
television
channel
TV programme
theatre

other nouns
job
medicine

verbs
find out
get better
give (something
back)
happen
have a meal
make meals
make a film
write a letter

adjectives
boring
busy
exciting
ill

18
work
businesswoman
engineer

135

internet
job
factory
meeting

names
Jim
Kim

places
city centre
London

time
a.m.
evening
half past
night
p.m.
quarter past/to

other nouns
conversation

verbs
come home for
lunch
finish
get up
go online
have enough
time
send
(messages)
start
talk to each
other
visit

adjectives
different
first
funny (strange)
last
online

expressions
Oh dear!
No problem!
My watch is
wrong
What's the
time?

19
question words
how
how many
how much
how often
how old
what
what time
when
where
which
who
whose
why

family
aunt
brother
father
sister

names
Daisy

the home
CD player
DVD player

places
building
town centre

time
every day
soon

other nouns
middle
noise

visit
surname

verbs
ask questions
find answers
make (someone
angry)
point
shop
stop (doing
something)

20
the home
address
address book
hall

leisure
instrument
message
mobile phone
text (message)
website

names
Charlie

other nouns
advice

verbs
ask (himself)
be sure
call/phone
chat
connect to the
internet
email
end a
conversation
get (a text)
go online
join a group
keep
make a video
open a
programme

pay for
pick up emails
save (phone
numbers)
say goodbye
sell
send a text
sounds like
speak
win a prize

adjectives
sure
worried

adverbs
often

21
time
autumn
century
fall (autumn)
hour
midday
midnight
minute
month
spring
summer
today
tomorrow
tonight
week
weekday
weekend
winter
year
yesterday

months
January
February
March
April
May

June
July
August
September
October
November
December

names
George

verbs
catch (fish)
fall
finish (school)
make (a fire)
make (a
sandcastle)
make (a
snowman)
sail
start (school)
taste
throw (a
snowball)

adjectives
awake
lucky

adverbs
fast
on the left
on the right

other nouns
wood

pronouns
each other

22
numbers
hundred
kilometre
metre
thousand

sports and leisure
cinema
golf ball
golfer
movie

family
husband
wife

other nouns
birthday party
birthday
present
ticket

verbs
become
climb (to the top)
film
get married
hit (a ball)
pass (a test)
take (time)

adjectives
far
tall

adverbs
actually
also
only
together

23
work
business
photo

places
entrance
exit

verbs
arrive
collect (tickets)

fall over
give (someone a lift)
have (a meeting)
hurry
join (someone for lunch)
meet
save (computer files)

adjectives
double

adverbs
after
already

24
transport
airport
bicycle
driver
helicopter
hot air balloon
lorry
motorbike
pilot
plane
station
taxi
truck

other nouns
adventure
money

verbs
be (in danger)
drop
get to a place
go by (bike)
go for a ride
go somewhere on foot
have problems
wait for

adjectives
curly
quick
slow
wrong

prepositions
without

25
names
Ann
Pat
Nick

body and face
face

possessions
flashlight
toothbrush

verbs
clean your teeth
go away
go on a camping holiday
have a snack
wash your hands

adjectives
alone
brave
dirty
furry
surprised
ugly

expressions
What else?
Wow!

26
the world around us
ground
jungle

time
during the day
most of the morning

sports and leisure
holidays
hotel
London
pool
tour
view

verbs
drive
go away
stay (in a hotel)
tell stories
think

adjectives
best

adverbs
next
now
quite far away
then

prepositional phrases
in the back of the car
on the front

expressions
Of course!

27
people
pirate

verbs
get ready
go home
go (for a walk)

hide
spend a long time

adjectives
lazy

expressions
Bye for now!
Really?

28
names
Betty
Fred
Lily
Paul

sports and leisure
adventure park
chess piece
first prize
magazine
rain forest
silver cup
website

verbs
enter a competition
explain
get lost
give advice
go on (a journey)
hope
lift
move
stand
win a competition

adverbs
perhaps

pronouns
(by) ourselves

expressions
Excellent!
Move out of the way!
Not now!

29

names
Jill
Tom

sports and leisure
baseball
basketball
bat
dancing
fishing
goal
hockey
ice skating
partner
player
sailing
skating
skiing
skis
sledge
snowboarding
sports centre
swimming
table tennis
volleyball
winner

verbs
bounce a ball
catch fish
fish
hit a ball
hold
improve
pull
push
race
skate

adjectives
popular

prepositions
across

30

sports and leisure
cyclist
snow sports

verbs
cycle
go up in a lift
sailing boats
take a taxi
win a race

conjunctions
because
so

adverbs
not yet

prepositional phrases
on the fifth floor

expressions
I can't wait!
What a terrible mistake!

31

family and friends
baby
grown-up

names
Bill
Richard

verbs
come back
smile

adjectives
awake
several

adverbs
always
yet

determiners
all
a lot of
most of

prepositions
next to
round

pronouns
everyone

32

places
bank
building
bus station
chemist
elevator
flat
market
post office
roof
shop
shopping centre
skyscraper
store

possessions
letter
postcard

the home
bathroom
bedroom

work
postman

verbs
change
finish school
go shopping
have a party
plant

adjectives
light
safe

prepositions and adverbs
inside
outside
under
ago
for
since

prepositional phrases
on my way to

33

body and face
arm
stomach

health
ambulance
chemist's
cold
cough
dentist
earache
headache
hospital
medicine
nurse
stomach-ache
toothache

the home
soap

verbs
break a leg
go (red)
have/take a temperature
hurt
lie down
make (something stop)
taste (nice)

adjectives
better
broken
fine
ill
normal
well

prepositional phrases
in future

expressions
Poor boy!
What's the matter?

34

sports and leisure
comic
the end
soccer

possessions
diary

time
afternoon
Christmas
morning
Saturday
Sunday

family
grandparent
parent

verbs
collect
get better
make sure
make us laugh
mind
plant
score
sledge
stay (in hospital)

adjectives
bored
full of
kind
OK

adverbs
at first
a little
only
quite
really
so (friendly)
still
very

prepositions
like

prepositional phrases
in hospital

35
materials
glass
gold
metal
paper
plastic
silver

wood
wool

the home
card
envelope
fan
key
lamp
mirror
window

sports and leisure
drum
toy

other nouns
bridge
spider

verbs
be made of
burn
come from
see (through)

adjectives
flat
hard
untidy

adverbs
often
usually

prepositional phrases
for a long time
in the middle of

pronouns
no-one

36
the home
light
mat

school
the opposite

verbs
mean
must

adjectives
first
second
third
enough
old
young

adverbs
downstairs
slowly
upstairs
down

prepositions
above
behind
between
in front of
into
past
through
up

question words
how long (does it take)

37
work
fire
fire engine
fireman
fire station
firewoman
police car
policeman
police officer
police station
police woman

places
city centre
slide

transport
traffic
traffic (problems)
visitor

clothes
boots

other nouns
age

verbs
ask for information
dress up
lose
slide (down)
stop
telephone
test
wait
work

pronouns
anything
everything

38
sports and leisure
football club

work
postman
ticket office

time
Tuesday

other nouns
noise

verbs
get into (a car)

get out of (a car)
make (a noise)
smile
thank someone

adverbs
earlier today
just round the corner
one day (in the future)

adverbs
so much

expressions
Excuse me!

39
places
clothes shop
sports shop
stamp
sweet shop

the home
cooker
fridge

other nouns
balloon
timetable

work
footballer
waiter

verbs
sell
shop
sleep in a tent

adjectives
expensive
lovely

pronouns
something else

expressions
How lovely!
How much was it?

40
animals
cat
duck
frog
horse
lion
monkey
snake

food and drink
lunch box

leisure
song
sound

other nouns
wood (forest)

verbs
could
film
put up a tent
wake someone
wake up
wish

adjectives
best
fat

adverbs
ever
quietly

prepositions
above
below

determiners
both
such

prepositional phrases
at night
for the first time

41
sports and leisure
costume
play (theatre)
treasure

family
grandfather

clothes
shirt
swimming shorts

body and face
toe

the world around us
the light of the moon

work
cameraman

verbs
count
look after
sail a ship

prepositions
under

42
places
swimming pool

food and drink
ice cream

school
sentence

verbs
change (my clothes)
dry (my hair)
have (a bath)
have (a cup of coffee)
have (a shower)
have (a wash)
spend (money)
understand
wash (my hair)
will

adverbs
already

expressions
Dear (Nick),
I have to go now.
I'm sorry
Lots of love

43
sports and leisure
skis
ski lift
skier
snowboarding

transport
cave painting
New York

verbs
call (name)
grow up
turn

adverbs
down
ever

determiners
all of
a few of
both of
half of us
a lot of us
most of
some of

pronouns
everyone
no-one

expressions
What fun!

44
the home
armchair
basement
radio
sofa

other nouns
invitation

verbs
choose (between)
miss (a bus)

adverbs
just

expressions
Help!
Nothing else for me!

45
time
five o'clock
leap year
quarter past
twice a year

places
railway station
train station

verbs
change (the time)
stay (in bed)
stop (at a station)

adjectives
missing
correct

adverbs
later

46
school
alphabet
board

the home
apartment
hall
living room

sports and leisure
board game

toys
doll

verbs
go out
study for an exam

pronouns
anyone
(by) herself

47
names
Grace

work
ambulance driver
dentist

verbs
come from
have a
conversation
may
will
won't

adjectives
married
single

adverbs
perhaps

prepositional phrases
at school
at university
at work

48
sports and leisure
horse-riding
hot air balloon
movies
rock climbing

family and friends
granddaughter
grandson
partner
teenager

transport
railway journey

49
names
Jack
Jane
Lucy

verbs
do an exam/a test
do some shopping

do sport
do work
do homework
make a mistake
make your bed
make sandwiches

adjectives
weak

adverbs
anywhere

pronouns
himself

expressions
Why don't you..?

50
places
circus
film studio
gate

numbers
million

work
band member
dolphin trainer
film star
golf player
horse rider
painter
train driver

daily life
life

verbs
agree

51
names
Anna

the home
balcony
DVD

places
computer room
dining room
sports hall

numbers
metre

school
home page
website
information

sports and leisure
dog sledge
line
ski teacher
ski team

other nouns
coconut tree
library card

verbs
improve
let

prepositions
since

expressions
Be quiet!
Boring!

52
numbers
metre
times (27 x 53)

body and face
moustache

nouns
bit
(a bit frightened)

verbs
forget
know

adjectives
ready

adverbs
quietly

questions
What kind of?

53
places
bridge
path

prepositions
opposite
over

verbs
go (past)
go (straight on)
turn (left)
turn (right)

numbers
millions

questions
How far?
Which way?

54
verbs
be in a race
feel better
hurry home
make me angry

adjectives
poor
rich

55
verbs
comb (hair)

adjectives
cheap

determiners
a few

expressions
Be careful!

56
work
waiter

sports and leisure
water skiing
word game

verbs
cross out

141

Irregular verbs

Verb	Past simple	Past participle	Translation
be	was/were	been	....
begin	began	begun	....
break	broke	broken	....
bring	brought	brought	....
burn	burned/burnt	burned/burnt	....
buy	bought	bought	....
can	could	—	....
catch	caught	caught	....
choose	chose	chosen	....
come	came	come	....
cut	cut	cut	....
do	did	done	....
draw	drew	drawn	....
dream	dreamed/dreamt	dreamed/dreamt	....
drink	drank	drunk	....
drive	drove	driven	....
eat	ate	eaten	....
fall	fell	fallen	....
feel	felt	felt	....
find	found	found	....
fly	flew	flown	....
forget	forgot	forgotten	....
get	got	got	....
give	gave	given	....
go	went	gone	....
grow	grew	grown	....
have	had	had	....
hear	heard	heard	....
hide	hid	hidden	....
hit	hit	hit	....
hold	held	held	....
hurt	hurt	hurt	....
keep	kept	kept	....
know	knew	known	....

Verb	Past simple	Past participle	Translation
learn	learned/learnt	learned/learnt	....
leave	left	left	....
let	let	let	....
lie down	lay down	lain down	....
lose	lost	lost	....
make	made	made	....
mean	meant	meant	....
meet	met	met	....
put	put	put	....
read	read	read	....
ride	rode	ridden	....
run	ran	run	....
say	say	said	....
see	saw	seen	....
sell	sold	sold	....
send	sent	sent	....
sing	sang	sung	....
sit	sat	sat	....
sleep	slept	slept	....
smell	smelled/smelt	smelled/smelt	....
speak	spoke	spoken	....
spell	spelled/spelt	spelled/spelt	....
spend	spent	spent	....
stand	stood	stood	....
steal	stole	stolen	....
swim	swam	swum	....
swing	swung	swung	....
take	took	taken	....
take off	took off	taken off	....
teach	taught	taught	....
tell	told	told	....
think	thought	thought	....
throw	threw	thrown	....
understand	understood	understood	....
wake up	woke up	woken up	....
wear	wore	worn	....
win	won	won	....
write	wrote	written	....